Ideas in History

Journal of the Nordic Society
for the History of Ideas

Volume 7, no. 1–2
2013

Museum Tusculanum Press
University of Copenhagen

Ideas in History
Journal of the Nordic Society for the History of Ideas
© 2014 Museum Tusculanum Press, Copenhagen
Cover design: Erling Lynder
ISBN 978 87 635 5424 4
ISSN 1890 1832

About the Journal
Ideas in History is the result of collaborative efforts among nearly a dozen universities and colleges throughout the Nordic countries. The purpose of these initiatives is to further awareness of research, resources and activities in the field of intellectual history in the Nordic countries as well as internationally. The journal aims to create a meeting ground for the study of ideas in historical context across disciplinary, geographical and institutional boundaries. Ideas in History welcomes interdisciplinary approaches to intellectual history at the same time it acknowledges specific traditions in the field. Ideas in History seeks a pluralism of methodological approaches to intellectual history: reflections on the field, historical contexts studied, subject matter for intellectual-historical investigation, critical understandings of relations between the intellectual past and present as well as the comprehension of culturally, politically and geographically diverse intellectual traditions.

Acknowledgements
Ideas in History is published with the financial assistance of the Nordic Board for Periodicals in the Humanities in the Humanities and Social Sciences. Ideas in History also wishes to thank the Department of Philosophy, Classics, History of Art and Ideas at the University of Oslo for its generous support of the editorial administration of this journal.

Manuscripts
Ben Dorfman, Editorial Assistant, Ideas in History
Dept. of Culture and Global Studies Aalborg University
Kroghstræde 3
DK-9220 Aalborg East, Denmark
Email ideasinhistoryjournal@gmail.com

Subscription
Museum Tusculanum Press
University of Copenhagen
Birketinget 6
DK-2300 Copenhagen S, Denmark
Tel. +45 32 34 14 14 / Fax +45 32 58 14 88
Email order@mtp.dk / www.mtp.dk

Contents

Introduction
The Baltic Sea Area as a Historical, Cultural and Social Space

Katarina Leppänen and Rebecka Lettevall

Historically, culturally and socially, water holds a double promise as both a uniting and a dividing factor. This is true about several seas, such as the Mediterranean, the Black Sea and Lake Victoria. It is also true about the Baltic Sea area, whose imperial and political history is lined with conflicts and conquests. However, the Baltic Sea has also been a unifying factor and a vessel for travel and trade. Archaeological remains show that there was intense contact over the Baltic Sea during the Stone Age. From a Swedish and German perspective, the Baltic Sea has for centuries been an important link between different parts of their domains. During the wars and conflicts of the twentieth century, people fled across the Baltic Sea to escape from violence, famine and poverty—a situation not far from the contemporary migration around the Mediterranean. In the aftermaths of the Second World War, the Baltic Sea functioned as an extension of the Iron Curtain. The reestablishment of the three Baltic States, as well as the reunification of the two German states and the democratization of Poland, contributed to the current perspective of the Baltic Sea as a site of unification as opposed to division. For the last twenty-five years, there have been several attempts to strengthen the Baltic Sea area as a region. Many actors, from the grassroots to top European Union politicians and leaders, have initiated numerous projects with the common goal to increase and facilitate communication, development and understanding, using commerce, arts and common policymaking as means to work for this purpose.

The re-emergence of the Baltic Sea region after 1991 occasioned researchers to define it as an object of a new academic interest. This has proven fruitful. Several larger projects use the region as a starting-point for novel research and perspectives. Some examples are *Nordic Spaces: Formation of States, Societies and Regions, Cultural Encounters, and Idea and Identity Production in Northern Europe after 1800* (2007–2012) and *Narratives of Europe: Perspectives from its North-East Periphery* (2012–2016). Another research project in this area is *Beyond the National Horizon: National Imaginary in Literary and Intellectual Exchange across the Baltic Sea c. 1840–1940.* Several of the articles in this issue of *Ideas in History* are part of this latter project headed by Katarina Leppänen, one of the guest editors for this issue.

Area studies is a general term that covers a wide field of different kinds of multidisciplinary studies, often based on the social sciences and the humanities and with the first areas that were object for such studies emerging just after the Second World War. The multidisciplinary research environments that emerged through such studies often result in an unexpected development of theory, as models and methods have been tried and developed in new contexts and generate new questions. It is not surprising that the Baltic Sea Region has become such an area of academic interest for area studies after the end of the Cold War. The new geopolitical situation after the fall of the Soviet empire opened up a window of opportunities in an area that had been considered almost as a non-area. As the director of the Centre for Baltic Sea Region and Eastern European Studies at Södertörn University in Stockholm as well as being one of the guest editors of this volume, Rebecka Lettevall believes the combination of perspectives to be of interest to the humanities as well as to the social sciences.

National and Transnational Perspectives

In the Baltic Sea area, many different languages are spoken from several language families. This is an obstacle in the process of cultural understanding. It is also not a new phenomenon. The fact that culture and politics are interdependent has been put forward many times. As the Indian-American professor of literature, Gayatri Chakravorty Spivak (2003), has suggested, from the perspective of the United States, a combination of cultural and political perspectives is crucial if comparative literature is to survive. Likewise, area studies need competent readers of literature to make sense of different cultures. The emphasis on transculturality, and a "'culture-sensitive stance' ... allowing for the differences between the literatures of heterogeneous cultures" (Nünning in Lindberg-Wada 2006, 43) can be used as a methodological starting-point to investigate the appearance of national literatures in relation to political and cultural power. There are also obvious reasons to transcend the boundaries of both nations and geographic regions. Few research projects try to grasp this kind of Nordic/Baltic connection by letting presumed differences and traditional geopolitical areas be the nodal points that spark new questions with the aim of *not* reproducing self-understanding of national differences. There are problems connected to the cultural and geopolitical division of Scandinavia, the Nordic, and the Eastern Europe, a division that cuts through the area. One example is *The History of the Literary Cultures of East-Central Europe* (Cornis-Pope & Neubauer, 2004–2010). This impressive work loses some of its value when discussing Estonian literary history because Finland (not in Eastern-Central Europe) is not included thoroughly. The Estonian national epos *Kalevipoeg* (1862) is fashioned after the Finnish epos *Kalevala* (1835), and the cultural awakening of the Estonian language culture bears great similarities to the Finnish one, which is nearly invisible in the work. Furthermore, Finland's literatures have also had trouble fitting into a Nordic/Scandinavian/Finnish/Swedish nexus. It has been difficult to include Finnish language literature in the Swedish surveys, where the Finland-Swedish literature, especially on modernism, obviously belongs. On the other hand, the literary circles in Finland were and still are largely bilingual and relate to a national context; often still invisible from a Swedish perspective (see e.g. *Signums svenska kulturhistoria* 2008 and Koistinen et al. 1999).

"National sciences" is a derogatory term used to emphasize the role of sciences in nation-building (Berger and Lorenz 2008). Most disciplines within the humanities and social sciences are obviously "guilty" in the nationalization of scholarly work as the national borders were often used as the unquestioned limits of research. Sciences were accepted tools used in the development of the inventing of nations as well as the imagined nations (Hobsbawm 1990; Anderson 1983). Thinking outside, without, or beyond, the nation is often difficult as it has become an everyday category through which more or less everything is sorted, virtually unconsciously. Since the establishment of history of ideas and literature as academic disciplines have developed in relation to the changing role of nation states, there is no general history of ideas or literary studies that could be distinguished from tainted national versions. There is thus no "better" science one to which one can return. What remains is the reconfiguring of both the sciences and the nations.

From this situation, the question arises whether there are alternatives to the national. Such alternatives could be the global, the cosmopolitan or the transnational. There is also a tradition of world history or world literature (Moretti 2000). Today, the notion of the global is a significant challenge to the national; around the last turn of the century some scholars have discussed cosmopolitanism as a solution to this conflict (Arnason 2006; Beck 2000; Beck 2006; Smith 1995; Held and Archibugi 1995). As this field developed and proved to contain many standpoints, sometimes contradictory, the transnational perspective emerged as a more persuasive standpoint. Today, the notion of the global is a great challenge to the national, but it can hardly offer a solution to the everyday practices in the disciplines of history or literature. World history and literature grapple with similar problems as the global does, although the epithet "world" has a much longer history in the humanities, going back to Goethe's *Weltliteratur*. That given, there is a long history of attempts to define, circumscribe, and justify, necessary selections.

Transnationalism is thus a term that best describes the perspective of the articles in this volume of *Ideas in History* on the theme of "Nation and Literature." The national has in no way played out its role in how literature, politics, markets, histories, and ideas, are organized and made meaningful, neither in the early twentieth century nor today. However, the national is not a sufficient unit to make sense of itself as meaning is always created in relation to other subjects, be it institutions, individuals, nations or international organizations (Ramirez et al 1997).

Marcel Cornis-Pope has described his purpose as one of "retrieve[ing] those areas of intercultural exchange that were obfuscated by nationalist treatment of history" (Cornis-Pope and Neubauer 2004, 4). The establishment and strengthening of national identities through literature was both a transnational project and a national one. At the turn of the twentieth century intellectuals in the Scandinavian/Nordic/Baltic area, in the 1920s termed Baltoscandia (Holt 2006, 9; Hovi and Kõll 1998), drew inspiration from a shared intellectual field, while carving the outlines of their distinct national identities. How can this apparent paradox, the creation of something truly and distinctly national as completely dependent on something transnational, be understood? The geopolitical changes, from a few great empires before 1809 to small modern, more urbanized nation states just over a hundred years later, was a challenge in the area not only for "new" nations such as Finland and Estonia, but also for "old" nations such as Sweden. Literature played an important role in giving value and legitimacy to nations in their incessant struggle for identity (Melkas 2009; Ohlsson 2002, 2005).

The articles in this issue use, as primary sources, texts circulated among people who were involved in the political debate, not foremost as politicians, but as representatives of the cultural sphere. These texts created, considered and constituted the frames of the nation and citizenship without being explicitly political in a narrow sense. What is gained by sidestepping the obviously political is the way nation and citizenship was constituted on multiple levels simultaneously, and where the explicit political level has been the interest of political scientists and historians. By utilizing a variety of textual media the circular processes of transformation between the local/national and transnational can be made visible. This runs counter to the idea that "the cultural materials at hand", in the nationalist construction, were "cultures directly encountered, given, and transmitted *from the past*" (italics added, Eley 2000). What is rather more interesting is to investigate how the "literary and artistic production in these areas involved negotiations of tensions between nationalism, regionalism, metropolitan influences and local patriotism" (Cornis-Pope and Neubauer 2004, 5).

Culture is often understood as the result of common identity. The primacy of identity can, however, be questioned and the chronology reversed and it can be argued that a shared culture is the prerequisite for a shared identity (Spivak 1993). A deconstruction of the causal order is paramount for studies of literatures and cultures which seek to move beyond national self-affirmation. What happens when the nation or the national are not taken as an empirical starting point in the study of national identity? How is methodology challenged by non-national approaches? What can we learn from including new sources that research has so far been less interested in analysing? A transnational approach could "discern common structures that otherwise tend to be regarded as unique in one national context" (Jonsson and Neunsinger 2007, 258).

*

Two lines of thought and analysis run through this double issue of *Ideas in History*. The first one relates to the question of nation and nationalism, while the second question explores the use of literature as a source in historical studies. Katarina Leppänen's article "Fiction as a historical source: Alternative identities in Aino Kallas and Hella Wuolijoki" combines these two strands by exploring how literature can be used as a space to explore alternative national identities. Leppänen argues that the literary text, through its complex depiction of realities, can challenge hegemonic national discourses. The use of literature as a historical source has, however, not been unproblematic and the article starts with a short discussion about the status of the literary text. Two works, by Aino Kallas and Hella Wuolijoki, are then analyzed with the aim of highlighting the diversity in national origin and class that can be found in fiction, and how this writing creates spaces for negotiating presence in the national discourse, following Jacques Rancière. Theoretical issues about how political and social theory deals with identity historically are significant parts of the article.

Anna Bohlin's s article "Fredrika Bremer's Concept of the Nation During Her American Journey" examines the concept of the nation as it is used in Bremer's *The Homes of the New World* (1853–1854), Alexis de Tocqueville's *De la démocratie en Amérique* (1835–1840) and Harriet Martineau's *Society in America* (1837). The article analyses their different conceptualizations of the nation, which has repercussions on how they understand the bonds of society. Bohlin further argues that the concept of the nation is used as an investigative tool to think creatively about what kinds of bonds that will keep the modern, democratic society together. Issues of gender, race, landscape and national literatures turn out to be of great importance. Furthermore, travel writing is discussed as a genre in which women, like Fredrika Bremer on her travels, could write with authority.

Jenny Bergenmar's article "Selma Lagerlöf, Narrative and Counter-Narrative: The Question of Sources in the Historical Understanding of an Author's Works" focuses on the tendency of literary scholars to premier major works, instead of analyzing a variety of materials. The Swedish author Selma Lagerlöf was active in several genres and media, as a national figure and author of "major" works such as *The Story of Gösta Berling* (1891) and *The Adventures of Nils Holgersson* (1906–7), and in the "minor" genres of autobiography and articles on the conditions of women teachers and professionals. In this article Lagerlöf is explored through more peripheral sources such as letters, (auto)biographical accounts, magazines and some "minor" texts in her oeuvre. Bergenmar asks what links between public and private events and texts appear when these neglected sources are placed in the centre of the analysis, and how this changes the narrative of the author's reception and significance. Bergenmar thereby contributes to a wider methodological discussion on archives.

Eve Annuk continues the inquiry into "minor" sources (newspapers and women's magazines) in her article "Emancipation and the New Woman in Early Estonian Journalism." When ideas about national independence and gender emancipation became part of the Estonian public discourse, the printed media had a considerable influence on shaping the debate. The article analyses prevailing ideas in both newspapers and the first feminist magazine *Linda* (established in the 1880s). Radical ideas spread through the press; the article analyses the conflicts between the nationalist discourse, often implying a traditional role for women, and the emerging women's movement, which sought to expand women's role in society.

The next article, Kalle Pihlainen's "Josef Škvorecký and the Historicity of Literary Texts," brings the question of emigrant literature to the table. Pihlainen, like Leppänen, discusses the status of literature as a source. Pihlainen asks how literature can be approached in relation to the surrounding culture without merely explaining that relation in terms of some kind of reflection. Emphasising both the contextual and the intertextual aspects of fiction, Pihlainen brings forth literature as a space for alternative ideas that do not already belong to the vocabulary of an era. Aesthetics can thus open horizons that go beyond the ideological limits of a particular time.

Kristin Rodier's article, "Can there be a postmodern nationalism?" starts in Derek Walcott's poem "Names." Rodier takes us on a journey through a postmodern landscape of identities, asking why national identity is given such weight at the expense of other forms of identities. Affects of patriotism and religion seem to be constitutive features of selves living in nations that are not easily changeable. How can postmodernism be brought to the living reality of nations without dismantling them in theory at the outset? We are legitimate in asking postmodernists, she writes, "what do we do about the seemingly legitimate claims that national ties make on us?"

Our ambition is that these six articles can offer the reader new perspectives on the interplay between different sources in the public sphere. The complex intellectual and textual patterns that cut through nation, language, historicity and spatiality can enrich how we perceive the processes of, on the one hand identity and belonging, but also the need to negotiate and renegotiate specificities and differences.

References

Anderson, B. 1983. *Imagined Communities: Reflections on the Origin and Spread of Nationalism*. London: Verso.

Arnason, J. 2006. "Nations and Nationalisms: Between General Theory and Comparative History," in *The SAGE Handbook of Nations and Nationalism*, edited by G. Delanty and K. Kumar. London: Sage.

Beck, U. 2006. *The Cosmopolitan Vision*. London: Polity Press.

———. 2000. "The Cosmopolitan Perspective: Sociology of the Second Age of Modernity." *British Journal of Sociology* 51: 79–105.

Berger, S., and C. Lorenz. 2008. *The Contested Nation: Ethnicity, Class, Religion and Gender in National Histories*. Basingstoke and New York: Palgrave Macmillan.

Christensson, J. 2008. *Signums svenska kulturhistoria. Det moderna genombrottet*. Stockholm: Signum.

Cornis-Pope, M., and Neubauer, J. 2004. *History of the Literary Cultures of East-Central Europe: Junctures and Disjunctures in the 19th and twentieth Centuries*. Amsterdam: John Benjamins Publishing Company.

Eley, G. 2000. "Culture, Nation and Gender." In *Gendered Nations: Nationalisms and Gender Order in the Long Nineteenth Century*, edited by Ida Blom, Karen Hagemann, and Catherine Hall. Oxford: Berg.

Held, D., and D. Archibugi. 1995. *Governing Globalization: Power, Authority and Global Governance*. Cambridge: Polity Press.

Hobsbawm, E. 1990. *Nations and Nationalism since 1780*. Cambridge: Cambridge Univerity Press.

Holt, K. 2006. "Hur nordiskt är Baltikum?" och "Svensk kultur sedd utifrån." Report.

Hovi, K., and A. M. Kõll, 1998. *Relations between the Nordic Countries and the Baltic Nations in the XX Century*. Turku: University of Turku.

Jonsson, P., and Neunsinger, S. 2007. "Comparison and transfer: A Fruitful Approach to National History?" *Scandinavian Journal of History* 3: 258–80.

Koistinen, T., P. Kruuspere, E. Sevänen, and R. Turunen. 1999. *Kaksi tietä nykyisyyteen: Tutkimuksia kirjallisuuden, kansallisuuden ja kansallisten liikkeiden suhteista Suomessa ja Virossa*. Helsinki: SKS.

Moretti, F. 2000. "Conjectures on World Literature." *New Left Review* (January–February).

Melkas, K. ed. 2009. *Läpikulkuihmisiä: Muotoiluja kansallisuudesta ja sivistyksestä 1900-luvun alun Suomessa*. Helsinki: SKS.

Ohlsson, S. Ö., and S. Tomingas-Joandi. 2005. *Litterära kontakter mellan Norden,*

Baltikum och Ryssland: Föredrag vid internationell konferens i Tartu 2005. Tartu: Tartu University Press.

Ohlsson, S. Ö., and Tuldava, J. 2002. *De skandinaviska länderna och Estland*. Tartu: Tartu University Press.

Ramirez, F., Y. Soysal, and S. Shanahan. 1997 "The Changing Logic of Political Citizenship: Cross-national Acquisition of Women's Suffrage Rights, 1890 to 1990." *American Sociological Review* 62: 735–45.

Smith, A. D. 1995. *Nationalism and Nations in a Global Era*. Cambridge: Polity Press.

Spivak, G. C. 1993. *Outside in the Teaching Machine*. London: Routledge.

———. 2003 *Death of a Discipline*. New York: Columbia University Press.

Fiction as a Historical Source
Alternative Identities in Aino Kallas and Hella Wuolijoki

*Katarina Leppänen**

"The modern animal is first a literary animal"
Jacques Rancière, *Disagreement*, 37

Abstract

History of ideas and literary studies are disciplines sometimes termed "national sciences" due to their central, and continuously important, role in the formation and consolidation of the modern ideal of nation states. Attempts to transcend the nation as the self- evident point of reference are methodologically, empirically and theoretically challenging. The article moves across this varying terrain, starting with an assessment of the status and methodology of literature as a historical source, continuing with a case study of two works by Aino Kallas and Hella Wuolijoki, and proceeding thereafter to a discussion of theories that suggest a development in the processes of identity formation.

Introduction

Why is it meaningful to consult fiction when studying national identity and nation-building when there are so many more straightforward sources: political pamphlets, philosophical tracts and declarations written by great *Landesväter*? The function of the written word in identity formation and nation formation has been emphasized both in theory and in literary studies (Anderson 2006; Said 1995; Bhabha 1990). In the cases studied here, I understand literature and texts not as artefacts or documents that had an impact only on or in their contemporary society, but also as still co-productive of, for example, national self-understandings. The literary text, through its complex depiction of realities, can challenge hegemonic national discourses. The use of literature as a *historical* source has not, however, been unproblematic. Therefore, the article starts with a short discussion about the status of the literary text, asking what texts can do. The following section offers a historical and

---

* Katarina Leppänen is associate professor in History of Ideas at Gothenburg University, and research fellow at Uppsala University.

political setting for the two authors whose work is activated here, Aino Kallas and Hella Wuolijoki. Both lived in Finland and Estonia in the early twentieth century, and were active both as literary authors, and in the nationalist and political movements of their time. In the third section Kallas's short novel *Reigin pappi* (*The Rector of Reigi*) and Wuolijoki's drama text *Talulapsed* (*The Children of the House*) are analysed. The aim is to analyse how diversity can be written in fiction, regarding national origin and class, and how this writing creates spaces for negotiating presence in the national discourse. Their life stories and literary writing raise, indirectly but importantly, some theoretical issues about how political and social theory deals with identity historically. This is the theme of the last section, "National Identity and the Question of Historical Development."

What Can Texts Do?
To ask what texts can do is to turn the spotlight on the performative aspects of texts. Both historians and historians of ideas have used, and discussed the use of, fiction as sources. The reasons given for using literature can of course be different, but very often it has been a case of letting fictive events or figures illustrate a narrative, to give it a bit of life. Quite another usage is to let fiction fill the gaps where more reliable sources are not available. Such pragmatic use of fiction can, however, be contrasted to approaches that allow fiction to take the lead and become a source on a par with archives, documents, relics and other sources deemed more reliable or truthful (Iddeng 2005). There is, however, a growing interest among historians, at least in the Nordic countries, in using different texts (popular press, novels, women's magazines) concerning the same event, to confirm or disrupt dominant narratives (Sturfelt 2008; Holgersson 2005). Henric Bagerius neatly summarizes the more positive attitude to literature in the book *Moderna historier: Skönlitteratur i det moderna samhällets framväxt*, by stating that "literature complicates and qualifies, rather than simplifies, our understanding of the past [...] It stands free from truth requirements and claims to objectivity [objektivitetsanspråk], and that is its strength as a source for the emergence of modern society" (Bagerius 2011, 19, 29).

Indeed, historians are often occupied with representativeness and truth claims, in a different way than historians of ideas are (Iddeng 2005). For historians, fiction has a limited function, and the text itself is interesting only as far as it says or does something in the bigger picture. For a historian of ideas, an idea can be expressed in a fictive novel just as well as in a philo-

sophical tract or a legal document. Still, there are other aspects that have
worried historians of ideas—one of them being the relationship between the
text and the context. In 1969 Quentin Skinner proposed a position some-
where in between the two extremes (only text matters/only context matters),
which has since become something of a matter of course for historians of idea,
but which has also led to animated debates both within the discipline and
between historians of ideas and literary scholars and philosophers (LaCapra
1983; Bevir 1999). Although Skinner argues that the theory he promotes can
be generalized to all kinds of material "work of literature—a poem, a play, a
novel—or a work of philosophy—some exercise in ethical, political, religious,
or other mode of thought," his examples are picked predominantly from
political and philosophical texts (Skinner 1969, 3, 40) This is not surprising,
since Skinner's objective is to find the best way of *understanding* a text, which
entails questions of purpose, intention and aim (of the text, not necessarily
the author). We can reasonably assume that political tracts intend to say and
do something, whether the intention is successfully achieved or not; one of
Skinner's points.

However, does fiction have *meaning* in this sense, and do we need to *understand* it for it to make sense as a source in history of ideas? The fictive texts
analysed below are chosen regardless of the fact that the motive or intention,
especially in Kallas's case, was probably not to contribute to the discussion
about "diversity in nationality," for which I am analysing them. This position is unacceptable to Skinner who asserts: "The essential question which
we therefore confront, in studying any given text, is what its author, in writing at the time he did write for the audience he intended to address, could
in practice have been intending to communicate ..." (Skinner 1969, 48–49;
Skinner 1988, 73). Iddeng, like Skinner, is open to the performative function
of the literary text, but the questions he sees as following naturally from this
approach—"What was the purpose of the text? How was it understood, and
what effect did it have?"—do not guide the subsequent analysis (Iddeng 2005,
433).

Rancière argues that both structuralism and post-structuralism tend to
universalize, and create grand narratives based on texts, and that in this process they lose sight of the events and names of the actors (Rancière 1989).
The creation of grand narratives of the people or the proletariat then become
anti-democratic in that they miss, or omit, the micro-histories that make the
macro-histories possible: "The grand narratives about the people and the
proletariat were in themselves made up of a multitude of language games

and demonstrations" (73). But should we, following Rancière, be looking for narratives *about* the people, or narratives *by* the people? In his own analyses, Rancière uses both classics like *Madame Bovary*, and the "little narratives" that make up the voices in *The Nights of Labour* (273).

Rancière's reading of fiction as politics sidesteps the question of authorial intention, yet reads literature as a political space (Rancière 2006). The political cannot be directly translated to the issue of primary interest here, but every national project is of course political, and engaged in one of Rancière's central concerns, the inclusion and exclusion of political subjectivities. Rancière's model includes three instances: *the political* is the conjuncture of two heterogeneous processes: (a) the *police*, which is the set of procedures whereby the aggregation and consent of collectivities is achieved, the organization of powers, the distribution of places and roles, and the systems for legitimizing this distribution; and (b) *equality*, which can be achieved through processes of emancipation. The regulative function of the *police* is, among other things, to define the borders of inclusion and exclusion, that is, who can be heard and whose ideas, demands, rights, needs, etc., are justified. Furthermore, *police* stands in opposition to *equality*; it does injustice to equality by its exclusionary function. Politics, then, is a process of emancipation and the challenging of the regulations of the *police*. *The political* is a stage on which the verification of equality has to take the shape of a treatment of an injustice (Rancière 2006). Literature is one such stage, and in "On the Politics of Literature" Rancière discusses the democratic shift in modern literature: "It makes visible what was invisible, it makes audible *as speaking beings* those who were previously heard only as noisy animals" and it "cancels the distinction between those who act and those who merely live" (Rancière 2011, 4, 13 italics added). Politics is thus a challenge of the prevailing order, whichever order that is, and cannot be given or constant.

It is in Rancière I find a reason for including the literary texts chosen here, in the sphere of nationalist politics. They challenge nationalist discourse by the space they create for the misfits of the nation, those who have neither the purity of origin, nor choose nationalism before socialism.

Living Diversity

In Finland and Estonia, the dominance of the nationalist discourse in the early twentieth century was strong and affected all reception of art. Artistic activity, which in itself drew inspiration from the great currents of Europe aesthetics, had to be remoulded and given "national specificity," so it could fulfil educative purposes (Alasuutari 1999, 230–31; Lyytikäinen 2003). It is then not surprising that all so-called book wars, i.e. public quarrels surrounding published literature, from the first Finnish-language novel, Alexis Kivi's *Seven Brothers* (1870), to the 1960s, were about the authors' (in)ability to correctly depict "the national" or "national characteristics" of the Finnish people (Sevänen 1999). Finnish and Estonian society at the turn of the twentieth century were, and still are, multilingual: in Estonia German and Russian were the administrative languages, while Swedish, Russian and Finnish were used in Finland. This is the time of Finnish and Estonian national awakening when many families changed both languages and names (Allardt and Miemois 1981).[1] This phenomenon is part of a cultural rather than a political national movement, which, as Hobsbawm has pointed out, happened later in the Baltic region than in the rest of Europe (Hobsbawm 1990, 104). During the first decades of the twentieth century Finland (1917), and Estonia (1918), became independent and free states, which is, of course not the end, but only one step in the continuing process of nation formation.

Comparing the development in two nations always risks either glossing over, or (alternatively) over-emphasizing, differences. The point here is, however, not to dwell on similarities and differences, but rather to treat Finland and Estonia as an area with some similarities in historical experiences, and with well-developed cooperation between the countries on issues of nationalism and culture (Koistinen 1999; Hovi 1998). In many cases the similarities stem from a shared history; Finland and Estonia were the eastern periphery of the Swedish empire and later turned out to be the western periphery of the Russian empire. In the nineteenth century the term *Suomen silta*, the Bridge of Finland, was coined to emphasize the connectedness of the two peoples (Kreutzwald 1862). Academics, refugees, manual workers and artists' colonies moved between the countries, most often from Estonia to Finland. Different collaborations and Finnish-Estonian societies were, however, criticized, because Finland often took the part of role model that Estonia was sup-

---

1 During the first period of the Independent Estonian Republic (1918–1940), over 210,000 people acquired their own surnames. Those of non-Estonian origin had to renounce their original German, Russian, or other language names and take Estonian names instead. https://familysearch.org/learn/wiki/en/Estonia,_Petseri_County_New_Surname_Register_Cards_%28FamilySearch_Historical_Records%29.The issue is in no way settled yet, in 2009 and again in 2013, the ban on some names has been discussed, as was the idea that "Estonization" of foreign names would ease the integration into Estonian society (mostly directed at its Russian population), http://www.baltictimes.com/news/articles/21918/; http://voiceofrussia.com/news/2013_08_16/Russia-s-most-popular-last-names-banned-in-Estonia-0372/

posed to emulate. During the 1930s relationships deteriorated, largely due to increasing extreme right-wing orientation in Finland (Rui 1999, 391).

Aino Kallas's and Hella Wuolijoki's transgression of national and linguistic borders in the early twentieth century was both a result of active exchange in the region and a necessity under the prevailing political, administrative and educational orders. Since the general academic reader cannot be expected to be familiar with the life and works of Aino Kallas and Hella Wuolijoki, two biographical sketches are included below. This should not be read as an attempt to determine the meaning of their works from their life, but is rather a recognition of the marginal position of both the Finnish and Estonian literatures in general, and women's positions within them. The idea of pure textual and intertextual analysis is still largely the privilege of previously well biographed authors.

Aino Kallas

Aino Krohn was born in 1878 in Kiiskilä near Vyborg in the Grand Duchy of Finland. Her mother, Maria Wilhelmina Lindroos, was headmistress of the first Finnish-language girls' school in Helsinki and her father Julius Krohn was a prominent figure in the Finnish cultural revival movement, a folklorist, and a professor of Finnish at the University of Helsinki. Julius Krohn assumed Finnish as the language of the previously Swedish-speaking family (Oksama-Valtonen 2009). Her elder brothers Kaarle and Ilmari Krohn became professors of folklore and music, respectively. The sisters Helmi, Aune and Aino herself were educated from an early age to actively participate in, and assist, the male family members, in their intellectual and political work (Leskelä-Kärki 2006). They contributed to the Finnish nationalist movement through education, both in concrete terms as teachers and indirectly through the production of literature, children's tales and literary criticism. In 1900 Aino married a doctoral student who was tutored by her brother Kaarle, the Estonian Oskar Kallas and moved first to St Petersburg and then Tartu. The Kallas family later lived in Helsinki and London, where Oscar worked as ambassador in the 1920s, after Estonia gained independence. They returned to Estonia in 1934 when Oscar Kallas retired. In 1944 the family fled to Sweden and lived there until 1953 when Aino Kallas (by then a widow) moved to Finland. Her novels and short stories are today a self-evident part of Finnish literary history (Laitinen 1973, 1978, 1995) and her works have been acknowledged and re-evaluated in recent years by many feminist scholars (Melkas 2006; Rojola and Kurvet-Käosaar 2011; Kurvet-Käosaar 2006; Leskelä-Kärki 2006).

Kallas wrote more than twenty short stories, novels and plays. In addition, she edited and published her diaries, wrote literary criticism, travel stories, and memoirs. She is often described as a Finnish-Estonian writer, with a hyphen between the national epithets (Olesk 2011). The hyphenation is apt considering that she moved not only between nations, but also between different nationalist movements. In Estonia Aino Kallas became active in the Noor-Eesti [Young Estonia] nationalist group, which was composed primarily of authors and critics who wanted to open Estonian arts and literature to European influences, in order to create a more internationally oriented national culture (Kallas 1918). Through her husband she was also active in the more conservative group around the journal *Postimees* [Postman], a rival nationalist organization that stressed the importance of Estonian folk culture more than foreign influences. There was a pronounced conflict between the groups, but also an overlap in membership (Laitinen 1973, 126–31).

Hella Wuolijoki
Hella Wuolijoki was born in the Estonian town of Helme and received her primary education in Tartu, where she became involved in the nationalist movement, among other things, "fighting against Russian teachers and German mentality" (Wuolijoki 1945, 24). She then attended an elite school in St Petersburg, and graduated, as the first Estonian woman to receive a university degree, from the University of Helsinki in 1908. She settled in Finland and married the Finnish lawyer, journalist and social democratic politician Sulo Vuolijoki (divorced in 1923); she made a career as a translator, journalist, businesswoman, leftist politician, literary author and playwright. In the 1920s and 1930s Hella Wuolijoki hosted a political and cultural salon in Helsinki, which was frequented by many prominent artists, politicians, diplomats and international traders, from both east and west (Tuomioja 2006). Through personal contacts she facilitated negotiations between Alexandra Kollontai, the Soviet ambassador in Stockholm, and the Finnish Foreign Ministry. In 1943 she was arrested for treason after having aided a Soviet parachutist and spy, Kerttu Nuorteva. Wuolijoki was released following the cease-fire that ended the Continuation War. The eighteen months in prison were spent writing, which was made possible by a regime that encouraged prisoners to continue with their civil occupation. After the war Wuolijoki was elected to Parliament for the social democrats, and was appointed CEO of Finnish Radio.

Wuolijoki worked with, among others, Bertolt Brecht (on the play *Herr Puntila und sein Knecht Matti*) and was closely acquainted with Maxim Gorky

(Deschner 1980; Tuomioja 2006, 166). Several of Wuolijoki's plays were filmed in Finland and one even in Hollywood. Wuolijoki's leftist sympathies were a hindrance for her career as a playwright and at first she was played mainly at workers' theatres; at times she wrote under the male aliases Juhani Tervapää or Felix Tuli (Koski 2000). The cinema adaptations of her series on the women of the Niskavuori Estate and its fate have reached cult status in Finland, and a contributing factor to her popularity was her ability to capture (what was perceived as) genuinely Finnish national characteristics (Koivunen 2003). Today she is, after Aleksis Kivi and William Shakespeare, Finland's most popular playwright.

Clearly, then, nation and the national, understood widely as encompassing nationalism, independence and culture, had a great impact on Kallas's and Wuolijoki's life trajectories. They lived transnational lives, and perceived themselves to be cosmopolitans or internationalists, which is highlighted and discussed in their published diaries and in some previous research (Hapuli, Leskelä-Kärki and Melkas 2009). Yet they grounded their cosmopolitanism and internationalism in the nation states and their enduring literary activity was deeply contextualized in the national, in a continuous creation of self, community, history and identity. One could imagine that the Baltic region during this period represented a cultural and linguistic melting pot where transitions between nations were common and easy. However, that is not the case. Certainly, both Finland and Estonia were part of the Russian Empire, and, the Finnish and Estonian languages are close (*Ausbausprache*, see Kloss 1952). But very few crossed the linguistic border with the same success as Kallas and Wuolijoki. To imagine a shared or common identity based on proximity and similarity is as alien as merging the Scandinavians into a group and letting a Dane represent "Swedishness." Another explanation for the successful integration of Kallas and Wuolijoki can perhaps be found in the then contemporary understanding of married women's national and familial loyalty, or lack of it. Legislation stipulated that if a woman married a man of a different nationality she had to assume his nationality in order to create harmony within the family (Leppänen 2009). Consequently, it was thought that a formal change of nationality would automatically lead to a change of national loyalty. However, I do not think this is enough to explain how they were able to capture and express the national in a way that was acceptable in their new countries.

Regardless of the great popularity Kallas and Wuolijoki achieved, their loyalty, nationality, and representativeness was also questioned in times of political turmoil. They represented something foreign and dangerous, especially when the political climate was becoming instable. Was Kallas, for example, a good representative of Estonia in diplomatic circles in London, or was she in fact, according to her "origin," a representative of Finland? Was Wuolijoki's outspoken political radicality a mark of her foreignness? One must keep in mind that the prevailing attitudes towards women (for example, being dependent on male guardianship and protection) probably enabled a choice between a wider range of available subject positions because women's political and national aspirations were not really taken seriously. This becomes an interesting point for further research.

Writing Diversity

The choice to analyse the two works *The Rector of Reigi* and *The Children of the House* must be justified—they are not the most blatantly political pieces in Kallas's and Wuolijoki's production. Both wrote much more directly political fiction, and Wuolijoki worked alternately as a translator, literary author, political journalist and a politician.[2] The two pieces are singled out here because they deal with issues of national loyalty and belonging in very different ways. Both texts deal with Estonia; Who is Estonian? Must one be born on Estonian soil? Can one "convert" to Estonianism, and what would that entail? Are all good Estonians nationalist?

Examples of how the nation can be written can be found in Aino Kallas's historical stories where the initial question about the relationship between national identity and history emerges. There is no doubt about Kallas's sincere support for Estonia and the Estonian, and her works are part of the creation of Estonian history and the formulation of national identity.

When studying national, or nationalist, literature, there is of course some kind of conception guiding our searchlight—we look for texts that say something about the nation. However, the focus should not be too narrow as it may prevent us from seeing alternative narratives about the nation that run parallel to the more stereotyped stories. In other words, the nation is not only written in texts that are obviously nationalist, but also in other texts (Kauranen and Rantanen 2009). Kallas avoids getting caught in a nationalist template, according to which the nation's history is written by demonstrating its purity and strength, sovereignty, or the people's unimpeachable morality. It is not

---

2 Wuolijoki's play *Law and Order* deals with the civil war of 1918 in Finland, English translation in Kelly et al. 1996. Kallas's, for her part, wrote many stories of the Baltic German oppression of Estonians, but only in the genre of fiction, see e.g. Leppänen 2013.

nationality that determines whether a person belongs to the region or not; instead belonging is decided by affiliation and presence, or characteristics that can be acquired and cultivated, rather than given at birth. This is obviously not an *un*controversial way of writing, because the peoples can be perceived as more or less legitimate inhabitants. The presence of Baltic Germans, Russians, Finns and Swedes was connected to shifting relations of power and domination. Kallas's way of approaching difference was not compatible with prevailing Finnish nationalist literary genres.

Becoming a Man of the People
Kallas's novel *The Rector of Reigi* was published in 1926.[3] The story is set in Reigi on the island of Hiiumaa, in the mid-1600s. It is based on a few short excerpts from church registers, court records and archival material, but Kallas also collected material by talking to the locals as part of, what I would like to call, her ethnographic method (Laitinen, 1995, 151–54). The narrator is Paavali Lampelius, a Finnish-born priest who worked as a principal at an Episcopal school in Tallinn. He is accused of murdering a student after a scuffle. He is freed from charges but loses his position, and subsequently he is banished to the periphery in Reigi and demoted to a provincial minister. He takes his young and lovely Finnish wife Catharina Wycken with him, their two children "had been laid in a common grave for the poor ... the plague-pit" (Kallas 1975b, 63–64). Catharina is distraught by the prospect of life on the periphery of civilization. Soon a young deacon from Sweden, Jonas Kempe, is sent to help Lampelius in the parish. Jonas and Catharina, who is much younger than her husband, fall in love, and before Lempelius understands the severity of the infatuation the couple elopes. After a lengthy search they are captured in the Åland archipelago. In his testimony, Lempelius wants to lay all guilt on Kempe in order to save his wife, and in deep distress he wanders among the spectators, just moments before the sinners are beheaded.

Melkas has pointed out the unusual male characters in the Eros the Slayer trilogy, of which *The Rector of Reigi* is the second book, who break the norm of the interwar masculinity at the time of publication (Melkas 2006, ch. 3). Another interesting aspect of the story is Lampelius's downward social spiral, which is a result of society/church failing him by repeatedly pushing him outside its realm. Although innocent, he is banished from Tallinn because of the ambitions of another priest who wants to replace him; the church sends

---

3 The book was translated into English in 1927. References in this article are to the 1975 edition (Kallas 1975a).

him the deceitful Kempe; then the church chastises him for not controlling his wife; and lastly the court and church do not believe him at the trials and take his wife from him. But where does the downward spiral take him? And what does it make him into?

The main characters of the story are all Finns or Swedes; this is the time of Finland and Estonia under Swedish rule; the occasional German reference also occurs. In the background, the Estonians appear as a mass rather than as individuals: the peasantry, servants, fishermen and townspeople. Only in front of the court are they named, Jüri the smuggler and trafficker, Kristi the milkmaid and Sauna-Ann, who all testified against the lovers. Still, the peasants play a decisive role in the story as a whole, because it is a story that can be read as a *Bildungsreise*, in which a man from the upper class becomes a man of the people through difficult personal challenges. Lempelius's story is thus one of transformation from an urban headmaster in Tallinn, to a man-of-nature who hunts along with locals and participates in the seasonal rural life. After his wife's untimely death he begins to tempt fate by undertaking dangerous adventures. Lempelius's mindset changes after a near-death experience when he struggles for his life with a large seal on the ice: "Thus I began to root out the hatred from my heart, as it had been an old tree-stump with roots stretching deep into the soil" (154). The final proof of his naturalization is that the locals begin to consult him as a wise man about the weather, planting, hunting and fishing: "And during my latter years, I have been visited by those desirous of council, seeking the one for fishing-luck, the other for hunting-luck" (155). The path to becoming one of the people requires an inner journey and the closer Lempelius gets to the local people, the more he finds himself at peace with himself.

Through the people and their folklore, a foreign clerical class can be destabilized. In the conventional sense this is of course a downward journey, Lampelius is posted at this inaccessible outpost to strengthen Christianity, with all that implies of civilizing work. But in the book it acquires a positive meaning, a transition from something alien to something naturally belonging.

In *The Rector of Reigi* Kallas captures the development of the subject Lampenius in interaction with the events, the environment and the people surrounding him. He escapes the control of *police* and equality can only be found in defying institutional power in the contemporary social order. Lampelius is not the only one pushing the limits of subjectivity in *The Rector of Reigi*. Catharina is of course also challenging the role of woman and wife in relation to sexuality and desire (Melkas 2006). Kallas's stories often deal with liminal figures, and the crossing of the borders of the intelligible subjectivities, those that in Rancière's terms are yet to become legitimate subjects in the political. It is as if many of her texts are asking where the limits of inclusion can be drawn, or how these limits can be expanded. In *Barbara von Tiesenhusen* and *Gertrud Caponai* upper-class women transgress their estate and ethnicity, both being German, by falling for men of lower classes.[4] In *Young Odele and the Leper*, the protagonist Odele really cannot hear what the leper at her gate is asking for, his speech makes no sense and it is "the growl" of someone outside political perceptibility (Rancière 2011, 4). She hands him the rose that he requested and suddenly "She saw that the man she had looked upon as a leper was of a race of brave and splendid humanity" (Kallas, 1924, 35). *Alien Blood* tells the story of a young maiden who befriends a sailor, who, incidentally, does not speak her language. Their child was born with "black hair and brown skin" and his children in turn become great adventurers. Even the human/animal distinction is explored in the shape-changing woman Aalo in the *Wolf's Bride*.

The lack of initial intelligibility, and the way the women of the novellas and novels come to include the silent and the foreign as full subjects, is of course in line with a Rancèrian argument. Lampelius's "fall" into the masses, who are only individualized and named in the face of power, is another indicator of the productive analytical force of looking at the limits of subjectivities, within and outside political (national) power.

The results or outcomes of the different transgressions of the borders between compatible subjects are not given. Some lead to death (all leading female characters in the Eros the Slayer trilogy) while other transgressions are a starting-point for a new way of life, or a revelation for the individual. Rancière's makes a point of the indeterminacy of literature; what is made available by writing and reading is not messages or representations: "What literature endows the workers with [in Rancierè's example] is not the awareness of their condition. It is the passion that can make them break their condition, because it is the passion that their condition forbade" (Rancière 2009, 278). Lampenius too moves beyond the activities fit for him, he moves into the forbidden condition of the people. If the Estonian and Finnish nations were to be created, it required this kind of rapprochement between the elite and the people, because one of the tangible problems in creating *a* nation and

---

4 English translations can be found in Kallas 1975; Kallas 1924.

a people was the presence of foreign elites, Finland-Swedes and Baltic Germans. While Rancière is primarily interested in the equality seen from the perspective of the underdog, the situation in the midst of a nation-building project could thus include movement in different directions where the socio-culturally lower classes embodied the desired characteristics.

Class in the Twentieth Century
If Kallas tells a story about the naturalization of a strange elite, then Wuolijoki's play *The Children of the House* addresses the problematic diversity among the ethnic Estonians themselves, and the insufficiency of nationalism as the all-embracing political ideology of a rising people. Socialism and class were central themes in Wuolijoki's works throughout her career, often illustrated as a conflict between women and men of different classes. *The Children of the House* was Wuolijoki's first play and it premiered in 1912 in Estonia, but the play was immediately banned by the Russian authorities for its national-ist content. Wuolijoki treats Estonia as an area distinguishable from Russia and an axis is established between Siberia, Estonia, and Europe, along which the characters move ideologically and physically. The censor, however, com-mented: "You cannot travel from Russia to Russia," indicating that the distinc-tion between Estonia and Russia was a dangerous one (Koski 1997, 220). The same mental travel restrictions apparently applied to Finland, where the play was banned on the premiere night the following year.

The plot circles around the children of two families, Mägiste (≈hill) and Alaste (≈down). It is "Time: before the 1905 events, Place: South Estonia."[5] The precision of time is important because 1905 is the year of many revolts in the Russian domains as well as a sharpening of the movement for independ-ence in Finland and Estonia. Marianne Alaste returns home from a four-year stay in Russia, where she has studied and worked, to find her family in financial difficulties. The family farm is about to be auctioned. Marianne had received money from her parents to cover her education, but had not been able to support them after she finished her studies. The neighbour's son Peeter Mägiste, whom Marianne had a fling with before going away, was now a lawyer with a European doctorate. He visits his parent's home in the company of his fiancée, the frivolous upper-class girl Julia Tranberg from an "upstart family" (Wuolijoki 1999, 8). Marianne and Peeter were once part of the same

---

5 Wuolijoki 1966 [1912]. This precision of time and place can be found in the radio adaptation (in Finnish), but not in the Estonian reprint (Wuolijoki 1999). The following page references are to the Estonian reprint from 1999.

Estonian national movement, but whereas Peeter has become a front figure for nationalism, Marianne has turned to socialism: The split in world-views is summarized in a tense altercation where the neighbours and childhood friends have been distanced from each other "Peeter: I come from Europe. Marianne: And I come from Russia" (22).

It turns out that Marianne has secretly paid for Peeter's education by pretending that the money came from his grandfather. When this is revealed, to Peeter's embarrassment, he tries to repay his debt by buying the house and all its contents in order to give it back to the family. But he acts under the false impression that Marianne will return to him as soon as Julia has left him. Marianne, however, can no longer see herself as his wife because the whole idea of nationalism seems too enclosed. Instead, she wants to move to Tallinn to work as a teacher with her brother Jaan, who is going to study, and Peeter's brother Hans, who is going to work in a factory. Marianne's choice is clearly, in the play, the progressive one, whereas Peeter's position is both outdated and immature.

Peeter and Marianne represent two new "kinds" in early twentieth-century literature. Marianne, on the one hand, embodies and acts according to the convictions of the socialist new women, as defined by among others Alexandra Kollontai (Ledger 1997; Kollontai 1918). Peeter, on the other hand, represents the upstart, a man of the people, who has earned money and acquired new tastes. The two worlds clash on a number of issues. Wuolijoki uses these to discuss the social and individual values of the coming Estonian society. The expectations of the socialist woman and the nationalist man on gendered ways of being is one insurmountable obstacle. Peeter simultaneously affirms Marianne's right to be independent, and, expects her to prioritize motherhood.

> Peeter: I will take you away from that group of wasters, world demolishers and brutes. They have filled that little head with gunpowder, and when mother Marianne carries my sons in her arms she will teach them real work [nationalist work].
> [...]
> Marianne: I cannot respect your work, I cannot work with you Peeter!
> [...]
> Peeter: You will see, Marianne, child, that when we two are together there is nothing else in the world but us.
> Marianne: That's not true, Peeter! You have your work and I have my own

work, and we live among people. And you insist that I should leave my work and my friends. (Wuolijoki 1999, 62–63)

Peeter insists that Marianne will become a "full-blooded woman" and bear him sons: "You are a woman, you should chose and sacrifice" (Wuolijoki 1999, 63, 66). Marianne rejects him again and again because their ideologies are too different "I would have to teach my sons to despise their father's work" (64). Indeed, she knew her "Bebel better than her Bible" (16) where women's emancipation was concerned.

A second clash of ideologies is between the solidarity of the socialist and the egotism of the nationalist. Marianne's reason to hate the upstart instincts is the fact that he has acquired "the world view of a social class that has no worries about bread" while she has had different experiences (64). The solidarity of the working class is international, whereas nationalism is simply national. "I have no fatherland or folk [rahvast]: But I have people [inimised]" (33). This is where political community is put to the test—how is the political defined and where does the *police* draw the line of equality? The folk (nation) and the people (the socialist movement) point to different interests, different potential social movements to activate, but also pose questions of equality and inclusion from different starting-points.

There is also an undercurrent of criticism against the nationalist movement's focus on education. Hans, Marianne's confidant and fellow socialist, declares that the upward mobility of the nationalist movement is sucking the life out of the peasant class; all they can dream of is their daughters and sons becoming rich "earning-machines" (Wuolijoki 1999, 30), that is, marrying rich (Germans) or making a fortune through their education (capitalism). However, "education is good advertisement" (40). This is harsh criticism of the nationalist movements in Finland and Estonia who had the education/ Bildung/civilization of the peasants as the cornerstone of their movement. Often children go abroad, Hans says, just to study, and care nothing about the local people. That is the egotism of the upstart nationalists. Again, the play is set in 1905 before the politicization of Estonian nationalism when the national awakening was still considered mainly a cultural, not political, awakening, which relied heavily on the idea of educating the peasant people and thereby bringing them on a par with the Baltic German elite. Just as in neighbouring Finland, the cultural movement was in the interest of the elite, the Baltic Germans, as well as the Estonians. In both cases the rural/local/ original connection was a tool for resisting Russification.

Nonetheless, the new woman socialist and the upstart male nationalist still share an understanding of what kind of people there are in the world: (a) those who *build* (nationalists); (b) those who *demolish* (socialists); and (c) those who *criticize* (but remain compliant). Where Peeter seeks to build a nation, Marianne wants to destroy a system. The upstart characteristic that makes Peeter an excellent nationalist—his ability to "pat the pockets and the heads" of the farmers "making them [believe that they are] the creators of Estonian civilization!" (Wuolijoki 1999, 20)—is a trait that Marianne has to fight in herself. In Marianne's eyes, solidarity and political activism trump marriage and family. This is one of the leading ideas in the socialist new woman ideal. The very moment when Marianne almost falls into the arms of Peeter, a political refugee knocks on the door and the spell is broken. She remembers her devotion to the more radical politics of *action*, whereas Peeter's engagement is always *spoken*. Peeter once shared the high ideals with Marianne, but now he does not seem interested in putting himself on the line, he is corrupted by money. The corruption, or wavering loyalties, of the man of the people is a recurring theme in Finnish and Estonian literature. The upstart is a boundary figure floating between the peasant/origin/people-past and the urban/estranged/elite-future, and it is the very liminality of the figure that causes social and political unrest (Melkas et al. 2009; Anttila et al. 2009; Henrikus 2011). When the peasants sought education, they were encouraged. However, when educated peasants started encroaching on the social, cultural and political power of the elite, the interest turned to disdain.

Still, the juxtaposition of men's political interests with women's political interest stands in total opposition to the Finnish national understanding of the nation as undivided by gendered interests. The historian Ilma Sulkunen (Sulkunen 2007) has defined the emergence of this national peculiarity as a need to unify the nation during the general strike of 1905 and the ensuing successful struggle for increased autonomy for Finland within the Russian Empire. Including women in the group of citizens, who shared interests with all other Finns (men), doubled the number of political citizens.

Discussion

The texts analysed here do not make an explicit point out of nationalist politics, yet they offer interpretations of who inhabits the nation, and they say something about the internal instabilities of the nation-building project by pointing to instances of transformation and conflict.

Kallas and Wuolijoki offer alternatives to perceiving the nation, and their texts perform subversive acts within discourse. Foucault's discourse analysis, to the extent that it can be treated as a method, focuses almost entirely on the text as statement among other statements/texts, and the relation between them (Foucault 1982). An important point for this article's analysis is the fact that the texts are highly different. Especially Kallas's texts have almost exclusively been read as love stories, even to the dismay of one of her contemporary literary critics (see Melkas 2006 182–83). Foucault, even when emphasizing the unimportance of the author's intentions for the analysis of a text, still takes an interest in mechanisms of exclusion: who gets to talk within discourse and discipline and who is silenced (Foucault 1977). The authors (Kallas and Wuolijoki) are important, because they make visible the variety of positions from which contributions to the discussion of the nation were produced. The ability to read them as contributing to discourse is, however, dependent on the position they hold. Foucault calls this "a rarefaction among speaking subjects: none may enter into discourse on a specific subject unless he has satisfied certain conditions" (Foucault 1982, 224). A disqualifier from nationalist discourse is of course the desire to complicate issues of the nation and its diverse peoples, to "paint rather than instruct" (Rancière 2006, 203). Much of the theory of early women's literature, postcolonial literature, exile literature, and world literature, is rendered meaningless if the authors' positions, even experiences, are not at all acknowledged. The fact that the texts produced by such authors have been essential in, for example, reconceptualizing genre boundaries, has emphasized the need to widen the concept of literary and historical sources (see also Jenny Bergenmar's article in this issue). Their contemporaries argued against Kallas's and Wuolijoki's ability to truthfully capture their nations because they were non-natives to their countries: "not born from Estonian soil, only replanted there," Gustaf Suits wrote in a review of Kallas's book *Ants Raudajalg* (1907, quoted in Laitinen 1973, 98). Paradoxically, however, parts of their literary production became important national symbols. This is especially true of Hella Wuolijoki's series of theatre plays about the Niskavuori estate (Koivunen 2003).

How should Kallas's and Wuolijoki's writing of diversity be understood? Their lives and writings span through the three phases of nation-building identified by Miroslav Hroch: from an apolitical cultural awakening, through the initial politicization of the nation and nationality, to the transition to the modern nation state. Language and nationality were largely a matter of choice, of representation, and the performance of a desired identity (Hall 1997; Butler 1990). They participated in the creation of a discourse where there is a space for contingent hegemonic re-articulations of political and national identities (Laclau and Mouffe, 2001). This means that what is created as a representation of national identity, such as character traits, must in themselves contain their opposite, and they are therefore both mutable and negotiable. Hierarchies, relationships of dependence, language and nationality, are not settled once and for all, determining what we are.. Rather, we make ourselves through our actions; for example, by writing fiction that depicts a diversity of historical actors, rather than emphasizing simplicity or purity. Writing fiction is of course part of creating what Benedict Anderson has called imagined communities, but perhaps it is even more important to think of literature as creating interpretive communities through which events and history gain meaning (O'Brien 1997, 5). This perspective brings to the fore the potential of a literary text to broaden the repertoire of thinkable answers to questions of who we are and where we come from. This means that I read Kallas's and Wuolijoki's texts as articulations of the intersections between being, becoming and representing.

National Identity and the Question of Historical Development
Why is it important to include a wide variety of historical sources when theoretically conceptualizing or reconceptualizing, for example, national identity? In this article I have tried to understand how belonging, sameness and difference are performed in literature. I don't believe that Kallas and Wuolijoki capture a variety of identities that exist, which people can adopt or refuse. The performative aspect is in their investigation of how a variety of subjects become social actors in relationship to other actors, expectations and contexts. Understanding identity not as a given characteristic of the subject, but rather as an ongoing becoming, allows for a perspective where, for example, identity change, or multiple identities, or layers of identities (the way identity is often conceptualized in current research, Bruter 2005), are of less interest than the social and political powers within which the subject is made intelligible. I will now briefly turn to discuss how national identity has been understood, by a number of historians and theoreticians, as a historical phenomenon. This summary review has the purpose of problematizing how ideas about the existence of different individual and collective identity has been used as a measurement of development, my argument being that a wider variety of texts may complicate a simplified picture of a historical change.

   The term identity is unavoidable in discussions of nation-building. Judith Butler's theory of gender performativity has led Merje Kuus to reevaluate research on national identity from a rewarding perspective. Identity, Kuus argues, is often treated as a feature of a subject. This leads to a "conceptual problem—namely, that the story by which identity is told is circular, presupposing the very subject for which it is seeks to give an account" (Kuus 2007, 91). Even though very few understand identity to be essentially given and unchangeable, many surveys and studies analyse identity as a necessary feature of the subject (91).

A great deal of social and political theory assumes that we have moved towards more complex societies with regard to national identities, and self-identification in general. For example John Urry borrows the theory of complexity from the natural sciences in order to explain the new "global complexity" (Urry 2003). A few examples: Chantal Mouffe and Ernesto Laclau dismiss the "prospect of a perfectly unitary and homogeneous collective" which has been challenged by the "plural and multifarious character of contemporary social struggle" (Laclau and Mouffe 2001, 2–3). From quite a different perspective (focusing on the individual) Rosi Braidotti poses "traditional" and post-modern identities as sequential: "the traditional unitary subject-position has become displaced under the contradictory pressure of global, post-industrial social relations" (Braidotti 2006, 30). Furthermore, a social theorist like Ulrich Beck argues that his theory of cosmopolitan subjectivities is something quite different from earlier theories of cosmopolitanism because it describes "different realities" and does not mean "uniformity or homogenization" (Beck 2007). The list of examples where traditional/unitary/simple are opposed to post-modern/fragmented/complex can be made longer and it follows from the Enlightenment idea of progress, refinement and complexity as characteristics of today rather than yesterday.

This line of thinking runs contrary to another way of approaching the complexities of societies and identities that can be found in Judith Butler's philosophy of performance (Butler 1990). Butler makes no distinction between past simplicity and present complexity. Neither does she distinguish between complex or simple contemporary socio-cultural contexts. Instead, identity, or in more Butlerian terms, subjectivity, is always understood as deeply embedded in a context, framed by values, norms and social expectations (Butler and Spivak 2007).

The above-mentioned theoreticians all emphasize the deeply political and contestable dimension of subjectivity, self-identification and belonging. However, neither Laclau, Mouffe, Braidotti, Beck nor Butler relate their philosophical and social theories to the historical sciences that interpret modernization and the formation of relatively homogeneous nation states as a *simplification* of social diversity. This line of thought can be found in the work of, among others, Eric Hobsbawm, Ernst Gellner and Benedict Anderson who, from their different perspectives, view the modern nation state and nationalism as a lumping together of diverse social groups, villages, language groups, nations, ethnic groups, into imagined communities (Anderson 2006; Gellner 1983; Hobsbawm 1990). This line of argument is evident also in the anti-globalization discourse that focuses on the homogenization of, for example, popular culture, and, the dominant position of English at the expense of local languages. The language issue is highly problematic in a field such as world literature, which wants to embrace the variety of literatures, but can only really do it in a few languages at a time (Moretti 2000).

What we are left with is an hourglass model: at the top, historical identity is something different from what we know today, diffuse in a sense; perhaps there were no subjects at all in the modern sense. Then comes the narrow waist of modernity, a simplification of identity, nations, easily recognizable collectives, that both social theorists and historians of nation refer to. Thereafter, the postmodern and/or global world makes it more complicated and the hourglass widens again. In other words, many theorists promote the idea that the development and refinement of identity *theories* is the logical consequence of an ever more complex *reality*. This understanding of the relationship between theory and history as co-developing is questionable for several reasons. Firstly, there is no proof that historical identities really were in any way "simpler," on the contrary. Returning to Kallas and Wuolijoki, nothing seems to be simple, neither lives, identities or identifications, nor literary themes. Secondly, we can see that identities today, especially identity positions posed by nationalist social movements, can hardly be characterized as especially complex: "Nationalist movements are instead engaged in a ceaseless politics of culture—an ongoing effort to identify, create, and maintain the purported common denominator of their national identity" (Segal and Handler 2006, 59).

My initial question about why it is meaningful to consult fiction in ideas in history is, then, that fiction as a source widens the perspective. Models that simplify the past and suggest linear models of development are insufficient in describing a history that includes fiction. New empirical material dislodges theoretical presumptions. Perhaps Rosi Braidotti is right in suggesting that there is no coherent way of understanding national identity; it is not opposed to globalization and internationalism, but they are rather two sides

of the same phenomenon. She suggests that we must disconnect the imagined interdependency between citizenship, nationality and national identity,
in order to be able to unravel their different meanings (Braidotti 2006, 79).
In other words, there is no simple correspondence between them. Potentially,
this allows us to think beyond totalizing explanatory models where there is
only movement in one direction, whether it is perceived as complex or simple.
With a more open perspective on both material and theory, it is also interesting to examine the idea of who and how national identity could be articulated
when modern nation states were established. The point is not to identify or
awaken an imagined and innate slumbering identity, but to keep open the
horizon for arguing about equality and universality, that is, the sphere of
literature as politics (Rancière 2006, 69).

In Conclusion

Approaching the issues of national identity and nation-building through the
world of fiction implies methodological, empirical and theoretical challenges.
I have attempted to address these in this article. Starting with the question of
what texts can do, I have analysed two different literary texts—the first one
using a historical setting to represent contemporary dilemmas (Aino Kallas)
and the second one directly addressing the contemporary questions of socialism and nationalism in Estonia (Hella Wuolijoki). Within the framework of
Rancière's theory of literature and politics, both can be read as exploring the
limits of inclusion in the political.

   What I have wanted to show is that, methodologically, there is an opening for using fiction as sources in history of ideas. What Rancière offers, in
this instance, is a theoretical framework of interpretation that goes beyond
the surface of the prose text. While the events played out in a novel can of
course be used to illustrate historical events, as mentioned at the beginning
of this article, that hardy qualifies them as sources. I make no argument that
Rancière is the master theorist; only that he offers fruitful openings for analysing Kallas's and Wuolijoki's literary texts as contributions to the politics of
national identity. Acknowledging the distinctive character of fiction as source
requires a theoretical framework.

   The analyses of *The Rector of Reigi* and *The Children of the House* are examples
of what such a methodology can achieve when applied to different material.
In the case of *The Rector of Reigi*, a story that puts great distance between
the events of the story and the time of the reader, theoretical tools are paramount. *The Children of the House* is also dislocated to the time before 1905, but

still falls into the modern period, which offers no great apparent interpretive dilemmas for the reader/analysis, yet the theoretical turn is just as important. What figures are activated, and what functions are they ascribed, in the processes of the ordering *police* and inexorable equality? How can questioning the prevailing order create new ways of being a national subject? What kind of politics do they perform?

The final overview of identity theory is an attempt to map a terrain in order to see where new approaches, such as using fiction as sources, could contribute to theory. When identity becomes part of the story of progress and development, connected to phenomena such as cosmopolitanism and globalization, there seems to be a tendency to make statements about lineal development. This article argues that in widening the scope of sources, such conclusions seem hasty. Using literature as a source requires re-evaluation of methodology, theory and an openness to new material.

Links

Kollontai, Alexandra. 1918. *New Morality and the Working Class.*
http://marxists.org/archive/kollonta/1918/new-morality.htm
https://familysearch.org/learn/wiki/en/Estonia,_Petseri_County_New_
Surname_Register_Cards_%28FamilySearch_Historical_Records%29/
http://www.baltictimes.com/news/articles/21918/
http://voiceofrussia.com/news/2013_08_16/Russia-s-most-popular-last-
names-banned-in-Estonia-0372

References

Alasuutari, Pertti. 1999. *Kaksi tietä nykyisyyteen: Tutkimuksia kirjallisuuden, kansallisuuden ja kansallisten liikkeiden suhteista Suomessa ja Virossa,* edited by T. Koistinen, P. Kruuspere, E. Sevänen, and R. Turunen. Helsinki: SKS.

Allardt, Erik, and Karl Johan Miemois. 1981. *The Swedish Speaking Minority in Finland.* Helsinki: University of Helsinki.

Anderson, Benedict. 2006. *Imagined Communities: Reflections on the Origin and Spread of Nationalism.* Rev. ed. London: Verso.

Anttila, Anu-Hanna, Ralf Kauranen, Olli Löytty, Mikko Pollari, Pekka Rantanen, and Petri Ruuska. 2009. *Kuriton kansa: Poliittinen mielikuvitus vuoden 1905 suurlakon ajan Suomessa.* Tampere: Vastapaino.

Bagerius, Henric. 2011. "Det moderna samhällets framväxt: En komplicerad historia." In *Moderna historier: Skönlitteratur i det moderna samhällets framväxt,* edited by Henric Bagerius and Ulrika Lagerlöf Nilsson. Lund: Nordic Academic Press.

Beck, U. 2007. "A New Cosmopolitanism is in the Air." *signandsight.com.* Accessed 9 January 2014.

Bevir, Mark. 1999. *The Logic of the History of Ideas.* Cambridge: Cambridge University Press.

Bhabha, Homi K. 1990. *Nation and Narration.* London: Routledge.

Braidotti, Rosi. 2006. *Transpositions: On Nomadic Ethics.* Cambridge: Polity.

Brown, Garrett Wallace, and David Held. 2010. *The Cosmopolitanism Reader.* Cambridge: Polity.

Bruter, Michael. 2005. *Citizens of Europe? The Emergence of a Mass European Identity.* Basingstoke: Palgrave Macmillan.

Butler, Judith. 1990. *Gender Trouble: Feminism and the Subversion of Identity.* New York: Routledge.

Butler, Judith, and Gayatri Chakravorty Spivak. 2007. *Who Sings the Nation-State? Language, Politics, Belonging.* London: Seagull.

Deschner, M. 1980. "Wuolijoki's and Bertolt Brecht's Politization of the Volksstück." In *Bertolt Brecht: Political Theory and Literary Practice*, edited by H. Heinen and B. N. Weber.

Foucault, Michel. 1977. "What is an Author?" In *Language, Counter-memory, Practice: Selected Essays and Interviews*. Ithaca: Cornell University Press.

————. 1982. "The Discourse on Language." In *The Archaeology of Knowledge and the Discourse on Language*. New York: Pantheon Books.

————. 1994. *The Order of Things: An Archaeology of the Human Sciences*. New York: Vintage Books.

Gadamer, Hans-Georg. 2004 [1975] *Truth and Method*. London: Continuum.

Gellner, Ernest. 1983. *Nations and Nationalism: New Perspectives on the Past*. Oxford: Blackwell.

Grad, H. 2008. "The Discursive Building of European Identity: Diverse Artic-ulations of Compatibility Between European and National Identities in Spain and the UK." In *Analysing Identities in Discourse*, edited by R. Dolón and J. Todolí. Amsterdam: Benjamins.

Hall, Stuart. 1997. *Representation: Cultural Representations and Signifying Prac-tices*. London: Sage.

Hapuli, Ritva, Maarit Leskelä-Kärki, and Kukku Melkas. 2009. *Aino Kallas: Tulkintoja elämästä ja tuotannosta*. Helsinki: BTJ.

Hinrikus, M. 2011. *Dekadentlik modernsuskogemus A. H. Tammsaare ja nooreest-laste loomingus*. Diss. Tartu: Universitatis Tartuensis.

Hobsbawm, Eric J. 1990. *Nations and Nationalism since 1780: Programme, Myth, Reality*. Cambridge: Cambridge University Press.

Holgersson, Ulrika. 2005. *Populärkulturen och klassamhället: Arbete, klass och genus i svensk dampress i början av 1900-talet*. Dissertation, Carlsson: Stock-holm.

Hroch, Miroslav. 2007. *Comparative Studies in Modern European History: Nation, Nationalism, Social Change*. Aldershot, Burlington: Ashgate Variorum.

Huntington, Samuel P. 1996. *The Clash of Civilizations and the Remaking of World Order: A Touchstone Book*. New York: Simon & Schuster.

Iddeng, Jon, W. 2005. "Litteratur som historisk kilde." *Historisk tidsskrift* 84(3): 430–52.

Kallas, Aino. *Ants Raudajalg* (1907)

————. 1918. *Nuori-Viro: Muotokuvia ja suuntaviivoja*. Helsinki: Otava.

————. 1975a. *Eros the Slayer: Two Estonian Tales*. Keuruu: Otava.

————. 1975b. *Three Novels*. Helsinki: Otava.

Kauranen, Ralf, and Pekka Rantanen. 2009. "Pilalehtien kansa." In *Kuriton kansa: Poliittinen mielikuvitus vuoden 1905 suurlakon ajan Suomessa*, edited by Anu-Hanna Anttila, Ralf Kauranen, Olli Löytty, Mikko Pollari, Pekka Rantanen, and Petri Ruuska, 221–254. Tampere: Vastapaino.

Kelly, Katherine. 1996. *Modern Drama by Women 1880s–1930s: An International Anthology*. London: Routledge.

Kloss, Heinz. 1952. *Die Entwicklung neuer germanischer Kultursprachen von 1800 bis 1950*. Munich: Pohl.

Koivunen, Anu. 2003. *Performative Histories, Foundational Fictions: Gender and Sexuality in Niskavuori Films*. Dissertation, Helsinki: FLS.

Koski, Pirkko. 1997. "Law and Order: Introduction." In *Portraits of Courage: Plays by Finnish Women*, edited by S. E. Wilmer. Helsinki: Helsinki University Press.

———. 2000. *Kaikessa mukana: Hella Wuolijoki ja hänen näytelmänsä*. Helsinki: Otava.

Kreutzwald, Friedrich Reinhold. 1862. *Kalevipoeg: Eesti rahva eepos*. Kuopio.

Kurvet-Käosaar, Leena. 2006. *Embodied Subjectivity in the Diaries of Virginia Woolf, Aino Kallas and Anaïs Nin*. Diss. Tartu: Tartu University Press.

———. 2011. "'The Vitality of Primeval Peasant Blood': The Hereditary Potential of Estonians in the Works of Aino Kallas." In *Aino Kallas: Negotiations with Modernity*, edited by Lea Rojola and Leena Kurvet-Käosaar. Helsinki: SKS.

Kuus, Merje. 2007. "Ubiquitous Identities and Elusive Subjects: Puzzles from Central Europe." *Transactions of the Institute of British Geographers* 32(1): 90–101.

LaCapra, Dominick. 1983. *Rethinking Intellectual History: Texts, Contexts, Language*. Ithaca: Cornell University Press.

Laclau, Ernesto, and Chantal Mouffe. 2001 [1985]. *Hegemony and Socialist Strategy: Towards a Radical Democratic Politics*. 2nd ed. London: Verso.

Laitinen, Kai. 1973. *Aino Kallas 1897–1921: Tutkimus hänen tuotantonsa päälinjoista ja taustasta*. Diss. Helsinki: Otava.

———. 1978. *Aino Kallaksen maailmaa: Kuusi tutkielmaa Aino Kallaksen vaiheilta*. Helsinki: Otava.

———. 1995. *Aino Kallaksen mestarivuodet: Tutkimus hänen tuotantonsa päälinjoista ja taustasta 1922–1956*. Helsinki: Otava.

Ledger, Sally. 1997. *The New Woman: Fiction and Feminism at the fin de siècle*. Manchester: Manchester University Press.

Leppänen, Katarina. 2009. "The Conflicting Interests of Women's Organizations and the League of Nations on the Question of Married Women's Nationality in the 1930s." *NORA* 17(4): 40–255.

———. 2013. "Political Dimensions in Aino Kallas's Texts." *Journal of Baltic Studies* 44(4).

Leskelä-Kärki, Maarit. 2006. *Kirjoittaen maailmassa: Krohnin sisaret ja kirjallinen elämä.* Diss. Helsinki: SKS.

Lyytikäinen, Pirjo. 2003. *Changing Scenes: Encounters between European and Finnish Fin de Siècle.* Helsinki: SKS.

Melkas, Kukku. 2006. *Historia, halu ja tiedon käärme Aino Kallaksen tuotannossa.* Dissertation, Helsinki: SKS.

Melkas, Kukku, et al. 2009. *Läpikulkuihmisiä: Muotoiluja kansallisuudesta ja sivistyksestä 1900-luvun alun Suomessa.* Helsinki: SKS.

Moretti, Franco. 2000. "Conjectures on World Literature." *New Left Review* 1. Accessed 9 January 2014.

Oksama-Valtonen, Hilkka. 2009. "Aino Kallaksen jäljillä." In *Aino Kallas: Tutkintoja elämästä ja tuotannosta,* edited by Maarit Leskelä-Kärki, Kukku Melkas and Ritva Hapuli. Helsinki: BTJ.

Olesk, S. 2011. "Aino Kallas on the Boundaries of Finland, Estonia and the World." In *Aino Kallas: Negotiations with modernity,* edited by Lea Rojola and Leena Kurvet-Käosaar. Helsinki: SKS.

Rancière, Jacques. 1989. *The Nights of Labor: The Workers' Dream in Nineteenth-century France.* Philadelphia: Temple University Press.

———. 1998. *Disagreement: Politics and Philosophy.* Minneapolis: University of Minnesota Press.

———. 2006. *Texter om politik och estetik.* Lund: Propexus.

———. 2009. "The Method of Equality: An Answer to Some Questions." In *Jacques Rancière: History, Politics, Aesthetics,* edited by Gabriel Rockhill and Philip Watts. Durham, NC: Duke University Press.

———. 2011. *The Politics of Literature.* Cambridge: Polity.

Rojola, Lea, and Leena Kurvet-Käosaar. 2011. *Aino Kallas: Negotiations with Modernity.* Helsinki: SKS.

Rui, Timo. 1999. *Kaksi tietä nykyisyyteen: Tutkimuksia kirjallisuuden, kansallisuuden ja kansallisten liikkeiden suhteista Suomessa ja Virossa,* edited by T. Koistinen, P. Kruuspere, E. Sevänen, and R. Turunen. Helsinki: SKS.

Said, Edward W. 1995. *Orientalism: Western Conceptions of the Orient.* London: Penguin.

Segal, D., and R. Handler. 2006. "Cultural Approaches to Nationalism." In

The SAGE Handbook of Nations and Nationalism, edited by G. Delanty and K. Kumar. London: SAGE.

Sevänen, E. et al. 1999. *Kaksi tietä nykyisyyteen: Tutkimuksia kirjallisuuden, kansallisuuden ja kansallisten liikkeiden suhteista Suomessa ja Virossa*, edited by T. Koistinen, P. Kruuspere, E. Sevänen, and R. Turunen. Helsinki: SKS.

Skinner, Quentin. 1969. "Meaning and Understanding in the History of Ideas." *History and Theory* 8: 353.

———. 1988. "Motives, Interpretations and the Interpretation of Texts." In *Meaning and Context: Quentin Skinner and His Critics*, edited by Quentin Skinner and James Tully. Cambridge: Polity.

Sturfelt, Lina. 2008. *Eldens återsken: Första världskriget i svensk föreställningsvärld*. Diss. Lund: Sekel.

Sulkunen, Irma. 2007. "Suffrage, Gender and Citizenship in Finland: A Comparative Perspective." *NORDEUROPAforum* 1.

Tuomioja, Erkki. 2006. *Häivähdys punaista: Hella Wuolijoki ja hänen sisarensa Salme Pekkala vallankumouksen palveluksessa*. Helsinki: Tammi.

Urry, John. 2003. *Global Complexity*. Cambridge: Polity.

Wuolijoki, Hella. 1945. *Koulutyttönä Tartossa vuosina 1901–1904: Juhani Tervapään yksinpuheluja aikojen draamassa*. Helsinki: Tammi.

———. 1966 [1912]. *Talonlapset*/Radio adaptation by Marja Rankkala.

———. 1999. *Juuraku Hulda ja teised*. Tartu: K. Laugaste.

Fredrika Bremer's Concept of the Nation During her American Journey

*Anna Bohlin**

Abstract

This article examines the concept of the nation in travel writing of America by the Swedish author Fredrika Bremer (*The Homes of the New World*, 1853–1854) compared to the accounts by two fellow European, liberal thinkers: Alexis de Tocqueville's *De la démocratie en Amérique* (1835–1840) and Harriet Martineau's *Society in America* (1837). The United States was the primary example of what E. J. Hobsbawm calls "the revolutionary-democratic" concept of the nation, but Bremer, Tocqueville and Martineau made sense of American society with references to the opposing, "nationalist" concept. Featuring national literature, the landscape, morals and manners, they also shared the belief that the United States had a crucial mission in God's plan for the improvement of humankind. However, they differ as to the significance attributed to the various aspects of the nation, as well as to what the mission implies. Furthermore, the "nation" may refer to different kinds of entities. I argue that this vagueness is due to the fact that they use the concept of the nation as an investigative tool to think creatively about what kind of bonds that will keep the modern, democratic society together. Their differences are explained by how they envision these bonds.

Introduction

Few would dispute the fact that "the nation" is a Romantic concept, a fairly recent invention of an "imagined community," in Benedict Anderson's words. Nevertheless, the exact content of that concept remains much harder to pin down. No doubt, "the nation" always has been a slippery and stretchable concept, and in the first half of the nineteenth century, it took on a whole range of meanings, that we do not normally associate with the nation today. In fact, E. J. Hobsbawm (1990) suggests that there were two *different* concepts of the nation circulating, "the revolutionary-democratic and the nationalist" (22). The revolutionary-democratic concept applies to a state of sovereign citizens

* Anna Bohlin, Ph.D. in Comparative Literature, has worked as a lecturer and a researcher in literature and gender studies at Uppsala University, Stockholm University, and Södertörn University.

that forms a nation, while the nationalist concept reversed the order and built on an idea of a community prior to the creation of the state. The tensions between these concepts were brought to the forefront by the discussions of the United States of America, a brand new nation and an experiment in democracy. Besides the French Revolution, the American Revolution is the primary example of nation-making based on the revolutionary-democratic concept. However, to European visitors at the time, that was not the end of the discussion.

The Swedish author Fredrika Bremer (1801–1865), the French lawyer Alexis de Tocqueville (1805–1859) and the English writer Harriet Martineau (1802–1876) travelled across the Atlantic Ocean to visit the future. They were among the liberal thinkers who went to the U.S. to find evidence of the benefits of democracy, while conservative thinkers went there to find evidence for the horrors produced by democracy (Runeby 1969; Wendelius 1985, 8–9). They also belonged to the first generation (1815–1850) that represented the nation with a reference to the past, that is, a representation based on the nationalist concept—the figure of the "awakening" national consciousness was first employed by Greek nationalists in 1803 (Anderson 1991, 191ff). The first generation of national independence movements proclaimed a break with the past; Anderson's (1991) most conspicuous example is the French National Assembly deciding on a new calendar—the nation inaugurated a new era. He also highlights the fact that the American Declaration of Independence of 1776 did not refer to American history: "Indeed, marvellously, the American nation is not even mentioned" (193). This did not prevent nineteenth-century European visitors from considering the American nation in relation to the past.

Hobsbawm (1990) acknowledges that the "two quite different concepts of the nation meet" already from the start during the French Revolution (22). Indeed, in Bremer's, Tocqueville's and Martineau's respective accounts of America, the revolutionary-democratic and the nationalist concepts of the nation are mingled to an extent where they appear to be inseparable. The criteria for nationhood was not a prominent issue in liberal discourse during the first half of the nineteenth century (24). Bremer, Tocqueville and Martineau are no exceptions. The chief concern of these travellers was not to discuss the notion of nation, but to analyse society for the benefit of their respective countries. However, in order to carry out that analysis, the concept of the nation was essential.

The aim of this article is to examine the concept of the nation as it was used in Bremer's *The Homes of the New World* (*Hemmen i den Nya Verlden*, 1853–1854), Alexis de Tocqueville's *De la démocratie en Amérique* (1835–1840) and Harriet Martineau's *Society in America* (1837). My focus will be on Bremer, who was perceived, by the Swedish women's movement at the turn of the century 1900, to be the great forerunner (Bohlin 2008; Bohlin 2013; Manns 2001); through them, her vision of society contributed to the modern Swedish nation-state. Tocqueville and Martineau inspired Bremer's travel, and the comparisons with their accounts place Bremer's idea of the nation in an international context, broaden the scope of the inquiry, and above all, bring out the differences between their different conceptualizations of the nation. They agree on the basic elements of a Romantic understanding of the nation: a vital relation to literature and to a certain landscape. Morals and manners lie at the heart of the nation, and are connected to the nation's higher purpose: the nation is a step in the evolution of God's plan for humankind. Bremer, Tocqueville and Martineau shared the belief that America had a special mission assigned by the Providence, but they differ as to the exact significance of the literature, the landscape, the morals and manners, and the assigned mission. As a consequence, they also differed as to how they treat the different indigenous, European and African nationalities present in the American nation. I will argue that these differences hinge on how they picture the bonds of society.

The bonds keeping society together were the issue at stake for social theorists in the nineteenth century, a time of social movements and profound changes all over the Western world. What they really needed to know was what brings the different parts of a society together and what makes them drift apart. What holds a community together and what creates tensions? Alan Kahan (1992) analyses the social and political thoughts of J. S. Mill, Jacob Burckhardt and Tocqueville—together they form a strand within the nineteenth-century liberal thought that Kahan calls "aristocratic liberalism." One reason for this label is how they picture the bonds of society: "According to the aristocratic liberals, the social and cultural leveling carried out by the Old Regime gradually weakened and even destroyed all the bonds that had formerly connected individuals in a society of orders" (16). The destruction of the social bonds places the nation in utmost danger; the aristocratic liberals warn strongly against modern isolation of citizens, against what Tocqueville terms "individualism," which they believe poses the gravest threat of democracy. The social bonds may weaken because people care more about themselves and their families (that is their natural bonds) than for the

large society (their social bonds); that is what an unguided democracy faces
(Kahan 1992, 17). *De la démocratie en Amérique* is a reflection on how to introduce democracy and rethink the social bonds, and still avoiding that society
will blow apart.

Bremer states in the preface to *The Homes of the New World* that her aim
was to bring the homes of Europe and the homes of the New World nearer,
"in knitting together the beautiful bonds of brotherhood between widely-
sundered nations" (the Swedish original literally translates as "siblinghood"
and "peoples").[1] Her use of natural bonds as a metaphor for social bonds was
no coincidence; it is essential to her social and political thinking. The bond
between nations also suggests a wider, welcoming community, but the compli-
cations are greater and more worrying than they appear at first glance. *The
Homes of the New World* is fairly well researched. Bremer's extensive contacts
with American authors are studied by Laurel Ann Lofsvold (1999) in *Fredrika
Bremer and the Writing of America*, and the major importance of the American
journey to the development of her feminist ideas is analysed in Gunnar Qvist's
Fredrika Bremer och kvinnans emancipation (1969). Bremer's views on abolition
are discussed by several scholars (Qvist 1969, 227–42; Wendelius 1985, 71–98;
Lofsvold 1999, 177–234). Lars Wendelius studies her picture of America and
compares her representation of the situation of American women, with the
very same authors that I will feature, Tocqueville and Martineau (Wendelius
1985, 57ff, 70). However, the concept of the nation and their ideas of the
bonds of society need scrutiny. Before venturing on the analysis, I will briefly
turn to the genre, the travel book. At the time, travel writing was part of a
scientific enterprise.

Travel Writing

Travel writing is today an expanding field of research due to the manifold
uses and ideological impact of the genre through history (see, e.g., Thompson 2011; Pratt 1992; Harper 2001). Actually, travel writing is an important
root for both scientific discourse and the novel; the interest in descriptions of
journeys to distant countries, fact and fiction, were heightened when Colum-
bus first set foot in America (McKeon 1987). The New World was not only
portrayed as the land of gold, but also the scene for imaginary perfect communities: in Thomas More's *Utopia* (1516) the story of the just and happy
society is told by a sailor who claims to have reached this land on accompa-

---

1 Bremer 1853b I:VIII; "att sammanknyta de sköna syskonbanden emellan folk och folk" (Bremer
1853a I, VI).

nying Amerigo Vespucci to the New World. The idea of the New World as a promise of justice and happiness goes all the way back to its "discovery." It is furthermore no coincidence that what is often considered to be the first novel, Defoe's *Robinson Crusoe* (1719), is a story of a journey and an exploration that turns into a one-man-colonisation; travel writing was intimately connected to colonial expansion (Pratt 1992; Harper 2001). However, this work of fiction also mirrors the increasing importance of travel books to natural history in the eighteenth century, encouraged already in the seventeenth century by the Royal Society and carried out in the eighteenth century by a growing number of men—and women (McKeon 1987; Thompson 2011).

Mary Louise Pratt (1991) stresses the importance of Linnaeus' world-encompassing system of categorization: the collection of plants from all around the world was instrumental to the scientific enterprise and was easy enough not to demand professional training (24–37). This opened opportunities for women to assume a scientific authority at a time when the only other way to raise their voices in public debate was through fiction (Harper 2001). Travel narratives constituted a considerable part of the scientific natural history writing—Charles Darwin's ground-breaking works are possibly the most famous, but not the only, examples (Harper 2001, 23, 94). An example from another field of scientific research is Tocqueville's *De la démocratie en Amérique*, considered a cornerstone in the liberal tradition. Tocqueville was still a young man when he travelled in America in 1831. The two volumes he subsequently published (1835 and 1840 respectively) secured him membership of the French Academy of Sciences, and later even a chair in the French Academy. The work is undoubtedly a theoretical treatise on democracy, but it is also a travel narrative, which becomes apparent on many occasions throughout the work.

When Harriet Martineau travelled in America 1834–1836, she was already something as extraordinary in the 1830s as a woman famous for her journalistic writing and successful popularizations of Political Economy. She was seen (by herself and by the public) as a "governess to the nation" (Hunter 1995). The outcome of her stay was no less than three books and an anti-slavery article, which "established her as lifelong authority, particularly on the abolition of slavery" (Hunter 1995, 9, 19–20). She also moved in the same circles as J. S. Mill, Radical in political as well as in religious opinions. Apart from the more personal travelogue *Retrospect of Western Travel* (1838), her travel writing was a scientific inquiry. Disciplines such as sociology, ethnography, geography, even economics were not yet formed as separate areas of inquiry (Thompson

2011; Poovey 2008). Lila Marz Harper (2001) argues that Martineau's *Society in America* and the methodological *How to Observe Moral and Manners* (1838) "were attempts to form the groundwork of a new discipline" (101). Her travel narratives

> transformed the nature of travel writing, making it a more focused inves-
> tigative tool of what would become the social sciences, a changing area of
> natural history where the provinces of sociology, anthropology, and polit-
> ical science overlap. In doing so, she also incorporated women's issues
> and concern for the domestic sphere into studies intended for a serious,
> academic, and thus assumed male, audience. (83)

Sociology would partially emerge out of travel writing, allowing a woman to be one of the discipline's "founding fathers."

Harper (2001) emphasizes the sense of freedom many women experienced when travelling far away from European codes of conduct and clothing, and even if the published account of the journey had to adhere to norms of femininity, the authority to make observations, draw conclusions, make assessments—that is, to assume a scientific authority—were accepted. To be sure, that authority had to be handled with care, wherein one should not violate the codes of femininity too obviously. The need to comply with norms of femininity had strong effects on the female writers' representations of themselves and the rhetorical position in relation to the audience. It also affected the relation to the object of study. Since the object of study in this case was the American people, both Martineau and Bremer were keenly aware of the risk to break decorum; after all, they had been invited to people's homes and their hosts were likely to read their books.[2] They were both right to worry—they offended quite a few, due to their frankness and, in Bremer's case, partly due to translation errors (Burman 2001, 349ff; Hunter 1995, 151). The object of study was subordinated to scientific goals.

Bremer was also a celebrity when she arrived in New York in October 1849

---

2 Martineau 1837 I, xvf; Bremer 1853a I, xff. Tocqueville also recognizes the problem, but does not dwell on it as Martineau and Bremer do (Tocqueville 1874 I: 23, II, 156). Martineau returns to the subject in the middle of the second volume and expresses her concerns for the paradox of examining friends: "Even now, having performed the voyage home, and having all manner of evidence that I have left the country three thousand miles behind me, I find it difficult to bring in my personal friends as elements of the society whose condition I am pondering. They are too like brothers and sisters to be subjects for analysis: and I perpetually feel the want of them at hand, to assist me by their controverting or corroborating judgments" (Martineau 1837 II, 136).

to stay in America for almost two years (Lofsvold 1999, 10–11). Several of her novels had been translated into English by Mary Howitt, who is reported to have learnt Swedish for the sole purpose of translating Bremer's books, and the English translations of *The Homes of the New World* would later be issued simultaneously with the Swedish edition. "Miss Bremer's latest!" was called out by newsboys in the streets (Kleman 1938, 2), hundreds of people came to see her when her arrival was announced in the newspapers, and she received an overwhelmingly amount of invitations to American homes. Her travel books exerted influence on how Swedes pictured America well into the next century and Swedish travellers to the U.S. referred to Bremer as late as in the 1950s, most notably in Tora Nordström-Bonnier's title *Resa kring en resa. I Fredrika Bremers fotspår (A Travel Around a Travel. Following Fredrika Bremer's Footprints*, 1950) (Lagerkvist 2005, 59, 71–72, 108, 208). One of Bremer's main concerns was to visit Scandinavian emigrants, who would pour into the country from the 1840s in increasing numbers; she recommended Minnesota, which was until then mostly occupied by American Indian tribes, as a suitable state for Scandinavian settlements (Runeby 1969, 18; Bremer 1853a II, 352). Possibly, this recommendation had an impact on the vast number of emigrants from Sweden, many of whom would eventually settle in Minnesota.

Bremer's *The Homes of the New World* is written in the epistolary form, not unusual for travel writing. It had the benefit for female authors of legitimizing the authoritative position by addressing a dear relative and to evoke the private sphere. Like the British travel writer Isabella Bird Bishop, Bremer wrote her letters to a beloved sister, who sadly died shortly before Bremer reached her home. The drawback of the epistolary form is that the integration of the private and the public sphere risked obscuring the scientific ambition—at least to the after-world (Harper 2001, 48–49, 139–140). The narrative, covered with endearments, is a study of society entailing contemplation of the nation.

Literature and the Nation

To the Romantic notion of the nation, literature is of vital importance: literature is the expression of the *Volkgeist*, in Herder's terminology. It should come as no surprise that Bremer, Tocqueville and Martineau found America wanting in that respect, since the U.S. was decidedly not a nation-state. Nevertheless, this did not prevent those writers from expecting a national literature and attributing a major significance to the national literature that they thought undoubtedly would appear. They disagreed only on the characteristics of the future American literature, suggesting differences in their respective notions of the nation.

Martineau adheres to the Romantic idea of literature as an expression of a people when she states:

> There is but one method by which most nations can express the general mind: by their literature: Popular books are the ideas of the people put into language by an individual. To a self-governing people there are two methods open: legislation is the expression of the popular mind, as well as literature.
>
> If the national mind of America be judged of by its legislation, it is of a very high order [...]. If the American nation be judged of by its literature, it may be pronounced to have no mind at all. (Martineau 1837, II, 207)

In her view, literature was not supposed to express an ancient culture, but the contemporary "general mind," defined as "the ideas of the people." Still, these ideas were actually already expressed by the legislation, which suggests that the nation was after all prior to the constitution of the state. Whereas Martineau argues that specific ideas will transform the literature written in America to American literature, Tocqueville expects a new national literature defined by its subject: the new public life. Democracy will affect the form and style as much as the content (Tocqueville 1874 II, 233; III, 89–98, 121ff).

Bremer, on the other hand, believes that she has found the "American character" in the poems by Waldo Emerson, but later changes her mind. The poet himself refuses to acknowledge that they "represent the mind of our world"—the true American poet is yet to come.[3] The landscape makes her reconsider. If she will not be able to see the poet, at least she will see

> his muse, the goddess of song which shall inspire him; have at least a glimpse into the grandeur of her kingdom, and the powers which she commands in nature; be able to form an idea of the life and development of those future generations which she will bring forth. (Bremer 1853b II, 90)[4]

---

3 "representera denna verldsbildning" (Bremer 1853b I, 170–71; Bremer 1853a I, 196).

4 "hans sånggudinna, som skall ingifva hans sång, få kasta åtminstone en blick i hennes rikes storhet, och de krafter öfver hvilka hon befaller i naturen, vinna en gissning öfver kommande slägters lif och utveckling i hennes sköte" (Bremer 1853a II, 101).

The muse is inherent in the landscape, which will foster the people, and the poet is thus comprehended as expressing the soul of the people permeated by the landscape. Before examining the function of the landscape, I will consider the function of literature a bit further. In Bremer's thought, the poet not only expresses the nation, but is assigned an even more active role, as becomes clear from a discussion of the national usefulness of the poet in one of her novels.

In *The President's Daughters* (*Presidentens döttrar,* 1834) Bremer pinpoints the poet's nationalist task: to "preserve the memories of nations; their fight, their victory, their wound, their acquired treasures." The nations "breathe higher and more freely" by the speech of the "genius," who inspire "actions of goodness and bravery" and encourages the people "when a nation bleeds" and its "liberty" is at danger.[5] The poet is no less than the creator of the nation's imaginary past, present and future. When reading the first national literary history by Atterbom, *Swedish Seers and Scalds* (*Svenska siare och skalder,* 1841–1855), she praises the "patriotic" qualities of the work and her "heart leaps with joy" on learning more about "the spiritual depth" of the nation.[6] To fully appreciate the significance of literature to Bremer's concept of the nation, it is necessary to take a certain kind of nationalism into account: Scandinavism.

After centuries of repeated wars, the relationship between the Scandinavian countries quickly took a suprising turn. Scandinavian people suddenly felt that they belonged together: they were siblings. There were even plans for a political union, inspired by *Kalmarunionen* in the fourteenth century. The Swedish and the Danish kings strongly opposed these plans, and after 1864 the idea of a political union was no longer an option. Still, the *cultural* Scandinavism prevailed, as Kari Haarder Ekman (2010) shows. The efforts to strengthen the bonds between the Scandinavian nations by individual contacts, by learning each other's languages and reading literature from other Scandinavian countries, were indeed successful, as was manifested by the

---

5 "Den odödlige sångaren, som bevarar nationernas minnen; deras kamp, deras seger, deras sår, deras förvärfvade skatter [...]?!! [...] Då snillet talar, då vidga sig nationernas bröst. De andas högre och friare; gerningar af godhet och tapperhet äro genom årtusen återklangen af dess ord. [...] Och då en nation blöder, då ett djupt sår blifvit gifvet dess hjerta, och det synes såsom måste dess kraft, dess frihet, dess ädlaste lif flyta bort under bödelns hand; hvem är som då ännu talar om bättre dar, som å nyo reser den fallna örnen och låter hans öga blicka emot eviga solar?" (Bremer 1834, 67–68).

6 "Arbetet 'Svenska Siiare och skalder' har för mig särskilt så stort värde emedan det är så fosterländskt. Allt som gör mig mer bekant med Sverges lif, som förer mig djupare in i dess andliga djup, låter mitt hjerta spritta af fröjd och min ande liksom känna sig större, mäktigare. Derföre läser jag åter och åter inledningen till verket. " (Letter from Bremer to Atterbom 9 February 1844, Bremer 1916, 387–88).

Scandinavian "Modern breakthrough." The reason for this successful peace project was Old Norse literature.

Scandinavism was *a form of the idea of nationality, peculiar to the Nordic countries*" (Clausen, quoted by Haarder Ekman 2010, 39–40). In the search for a national identity in the literary history, Icelandic, Swedish, Danish, and Norwegian scholars ended up with the same corpus: the Old Norse literature. To Bremer, who was born in Finland at a time when Finland and Sweden were still united in the same realm, who deplored the division of that realm and who stayed for a long period of time in Norway and in Denmark, cultural Scandinavism was a dear project (Stenqvist and Furuland 2009; Haarder Ekman 2010). The Eddic poems and the sagas remained a vital inspiration throughout Bremer's career, she even tried to learn Icelandic with her Danish friends (Haarder Ekman 2010, 158). In *The Homes of the New World* the ideas of Scandinavism are present everywhere; she jokingly calls herself "Viking" on many occasions. Consequently, the nation in Bremer's vocabulary may well refer to the whole area of Scandinavia, which sometimes included Finland, sometimes Denmark, whose border towards Germany was the cause of an armed conflict (Haarder Ekman 2010). To complicate the matter even further, the nation at times seems to refer to the provinces within the kingdom of Sweden. Bremer expects that it would "awaken national life and consciousness" (Bremer 1853b II, 389) if Sweden should learn from the American system of representation and invite the different provinces with their different peculiarities to be represented and acknowledged in the rule of the state.[7] As we shall see, she is not alone in making use of this vague terminology. Regardless of whether the concept refers to Scandinavia, Sweden or a province, the nation maintains an essential connection to the landscape in Bremer's thought.

The Landscape and the Nation
The concept of the nation is linked to territory, since the nation is equated with the state (Hobsbawm 1990, 19). The territory, however, may take on different meanings. To Bremer, the relation between landscape and nation is intimate: they practically define each other. Nature breeds the people and the people's expression through literature, and conversely, nature acquires meaning through stories. The past of the nation preserved in the literature is lacking in America, Bremer claims. In accordance with the ideals of Scandinavism, she deplores the absence in America of "an antiquity full of song and

---

7 "väcka nationelt lif" (Bremer 1853a II, 432–33).

saga, of glorious prophecy and symbolism, of gods and heroes who gave to Scandinavia so large, so peculiar, so romantic a life."[8]
The inscription of the past in the landscape is even more obvious in another passage where Bremer returns to this deficiency of the American landscape. She misses

> the life of sagas and traditions which we possess everywhere in Sweden, and which converts it into a poetic soil full of symbolical runes, in forests, and mountain, and meadow, by the streams and the lakes, nay, which gives life to every stone, significance to every mound.[9]

The "poetic soil" of the nation's past, that brings stones and mounds into the community of the living nation, is corresponded by the future of the American landscape. Bremer praises the fact that the names of the cities of the Old World are replaced to the new; this is a prophesy of the great meeting of nations that will take place in the New World and that will resurrect the life of the Old World (Bremer 1853a II, 205). Obviously, she fails to take into account the indigenous histories and names.

Martineau does not make the same mistake—she reflects repeatedly on the fact that the Indians preceded the Europeans, for example at "the Hawk's Nest," a high cliff with a spectacular view of the landscape. This "Nature's throne" is the cliché scenery for the trope of the sublime, and a much appreciated figure in travel writing, especially during the imperial era; Pratt (1992) calls it "the monarch-of-all-I-survey" (201ff). Martineau does not miss the opportunity to elaborate on the sense of power connected to the view. The place is supposed to have been "discovered" by a European, which Martineau finds ridiculous:

> But how many Indians knew it before? [...] Perhaps one of these may have stood there to see the summer storm careering below; to feel that his foothold was too lofty to be shaken by the thunder-peals that burst beneath; to trace the quiverings of the lightning's afar, while the heaven was clear above his own head. Perhaps this was the stand chosen by the

---

8 Bremer 1853b III: 261; "den forntid, full af sång och saga, af herrlig profetia och symbolik, af gudar och hjeltar, som ger Skandinavien ett så stort, så egendomligt och så romantiskt lif" (Bremer 1854a III, 297–98).

9 Bremer 1853b I:64; "det lif af sagor och legender, som vi ega öfverallt i Sverige, och som gör vårt land till en poetisk jord, full af symboliska runor i skog, berg och mark, vid strömmar och sjöar; ja, som ger lif åt hvar sten, betydelse åt hvar tufva" (Bremer 1853a I, 72).

last Indian, from which to cast his lingering glance upon the glorious regions from which the white intruders were driving his race. If so, here he must have pined and died, or hence he must have cast himself down. I cannot conceive that from this spot any man could turn away, to go into exile. (Martineau 1837 I, 125)

Untouched by nature's intimidating force, this spot grants superiority over the landscape and, by extension, over men; the superior position engenders a reflection on the political power of the "wild monarchs," now coming to an end. I will return Martineau's views on the exile later, but what I want to point out here is the past inscribed in the nature, the significance of the cliff and the surrounding landscape. The sublime Indian was well-used figure at the time, but in this passage it serves the purpose of connecting the history of nations to a specific land. Of course, the nation in this case is not the same that now governs the Hawk's Nest.

Shelagh Hunter (1995) studies Martineau's career and the development of her religious beliefs from a Unitarian background to a positivistic position, embracing a "Christ-based moral"—from "Natural Theology" to "Natural Science" (197, 102). According to Hunter, *Society in America* marks the politization of Martineau's Christian beliefs (194), but the more rationalistic apprehension of nature, in comparison with Bremer, is above all a legacy from the Unitarian emphasis on reason and rationality. Nature is everywhere: "Her forces are at work wherever there is mechanism; and man only directs them to his particular purpose" (Martineau 1837 II, 26). She invokes the "natural laws" even when it comes to tariff legislation and puts her faith in a rational development: justice will always prevail in the end, simply because it is rational (Martineau 1837 II, 30). Even so, the landscape is hardly devoid of meaning.

Hunter (1995) argues that Romantic ideas, in particular Wordsworth's moral psychology, remain paramount to Martineau's views on politics, morals and society. Wordsworth also influenced her apprehension of nature as a readable book (p. 146f). A Romantic Nature with capital N operates in Martineau's expression of her fascination on watching the Niagara Falls:

I saw something of the process of creating the natural globe in the depths of the largest explored cave in the world. In its depths, in this noiseless workshop, was Nature employed with her blind and dumb agents, fashioning mysteries which the earthquake of a thousand years hence may bring to light, to give man a new sense of the shortness of his life. (Martineau 1837 I, 108)

The newness of the very landscape, matching the new human institutions, is a recurrent theme in both Martineau and Bremer. In America, the creation of the world is happening under their eyes. "This was seeing world-making," as Martineau puts it (Martineau 1837 I, 109). Even though Martineau later left her Christian faith, she never lost faith in the Bible as a moral example. Her entire authorship is permeated by Biblical language (Hunter 1995). In this last respect, she resembles Bremer who, despite a keen interest in ecumenicalism, never abandoned her Protestant faith. In relation to the American landscape, they both employ Biblical references to formulate its novelty and grandeur. The American landscape might not be a "poetic soil," but it may certainly foster a new nation.

In Bremer's account, the American landscape is a condition for an improved human race:

That which is refreshing and new is in the various characters of the States represented, especially in those of the vast and half-unknown land of the West, *and the view over the wilderness and paradise...provide all the conditions for the development of a perfect mankind.* (Bremer 1853b II, 103. The English translation of the latter half of the last sentence does not correspond to the Swedish original and is therefore amended. The alterations are italicized.)[10]

Bremer writes the passage above before she actually visits the West and she eventually modified her opinion, but her expectations show the goal for her search for "the new." The political life in Washington, the battles and hostilities between parties, were all previously known from the Old World, she argues. The new is the natural scenery for a confrontation with the vital questions for human life in a gathering of different characters. The West is the place for a union of all people in a mighty landscape (Bremer 1853a I, 285–84). In another letter she specifies that her aim in the West is to study

---

10 "Det förfriskande och nya kommer af de representerade staternas olika karakterer, kommer i synnerhet från Vesterna stora, halft obekanta land, och utsigten öfver dess vildmarker och paradis [...] gifva alla de naturliga villkoren för utvecklande af en fullkomlig mensklighet" (Bremer 1853 SwII: 116–17).

the nature of "the growth, the Progress," which she believes to be the most peculiar phenomenon of the American community.[11] The landscape is the key to the future, according to Bremer.

Bremer conforms to a long tradition of picturing foreign destinations and America in particular as an edenic garden (Pratt 1992; Runeby 1969, 15ff; Wendelius 1985: 7). In the following quote, the paradise metaphor becomes significantly elaborated upon:

> The people of Europe pour in through the cities of the eastern coast. Those are the portals of the outer court; but the West is the garden where the rivers carry along with them gold, and where stands the tree of life and of death. There the tongue of the serpent and the voice of God are again heard by a new humanity.[12]

This is the "promised land, this land of the future" ("löftets land, framtidens land," Bremer 1853a II, 182), Bremer exclaims. Martineau, on the other hand, issues a warning. Her assessment of the amazing wilderness of the West is that the traveller may be lost "in reflection": "His old experience is all reversed...Nature is there the empress, not the handmaid" (Martineau 1837 I, 107). When she reaches the great lakes of Huron and Michigan, however, only a Biblical imagery can cover the experience: she is certain that the scenery is no different from the earth "the first bright morning after the deluge" (Martineau 1837 I, 195).

Bremer finally finds paradise, not in the West, but in Cuba. She wants to explore the natural conditions for the future development of mankind under "the warmest rays of the sun" and the Spanish rule (Bremer 1854a III, 217–18, 258). Although the wonderful air makes people gentle and the comfortable climate delights the senses, the political system and, above all the slave trade, contaminate life. Slavery is the snake in the Paradise. In the end, she partly blames the sensuous climate:

> People come to this beautiful island, like parasites, merely to suck its life and live at its expense. But it avenges itself, flings around *them* its

---

11 "fenomenet af den amerikanska samhällsbildningen i dess största märkvärdighet, som man vanligen kallar 'groth [sic], Progress'" (Bremer 1853 SwII, 172).

12 Bremer 1853b II, 161; "Genom östra kust-städerna inströmmar Europas folk. De utgöra förgårdens portar. Men vestern är den stora lustgården, der de stora floderna gå, der lifvets och dödens träd stå, der ormens tunga och Guds röst skola höras på nytt, för nya menniskopar" (Bremer 1853 SwII, 182).

hundred-fold, oppressive, snake-like arms, drags them down, suffocates their higher life, and changes them into a corpse in its embrace.[13]

Here she echoes Tocqueville, who would not consider Central and South America as part of the land of the future on the grounds of the climate:

Underneath this brilliant exterior death was concealed. But the air of these climates had so enervating an influence that man, absorbed by the present enjoyment, was rendered regardless of the future.[14]

The division is clear: the North is the home of the spirit, while the South is the home of the senses (Tocqueville 1874 I, 32) Bremer, for her part, still believes that this paradise on earth could be brought closer to its counterpart in Heaven if only the Spanish rule was abolished and Cuba became part of the U.S. (Bremer 1854a III, 300).

The conclusion is that the landscape needs to be supported by the social order. Bremer leaves Cuba, thankful for its revitalizing effect, but determined that she could never live where there is no freedom. Lack of a conscientious handling of freedom is also the disappointment in the West; "Freedom is still sowing its wild oats here."[15] Tocqueville agrees:

Their passions are more intense; their religious morality less authoritative; and their convictions less secure. The inhabitants exercise no sort of control over their fellow-citizens, for they are scarcely acquainted with each other. The nations of the West display, to a certain extent, inexperience and the rude habits of a people in its infancy.[16]

The West cannot yet fulfil its promise to become the home of true liberty.

---

13 Bremer 1853b III, 178; "Menniskan kommer till den sköna ön lik parasiten, som vill blott suga dess natures lif och lefva på dess bekostnad; naturen hämnar sig, slingrar sig med hundrade armar kring menniskan, neddrager henne, qväfver hennes högre lif, och förvandlar henne till ett lik uti sin famn" (Bremer 1854a III: 203–4).

14 Tocqueville 2006 I, ch. I; "La mort était cachée sous ce manteau brillant; mais on ne l'apercevait point alors, et il régnait d'ailleurs dans l'air de ces climats je ne sais quelle influence énervante qui attachait l'homme au présent et le rendait insouciant de l'avenir" (Tocqueville 1874 I, 32).

15 Bremer 1853b III, 235; "Friheten är här ännu i sina slyngelår" (Bremer 1854a III, 268).

16 Tocqueville 2006 I, XVII part IV; "Parmi eux, les passions sont plus violentes, la morale religieuse moins puissante, les idées moins arrêtées. Les hommes n'y exercent aucun contrôle les uns sur les autres, car ils se connaissent à peine. Les nations de l'Ouest montrent donc, jusqu'à un certain point, l'inexpérience et les habitudes déréglées des peuples naissants" (Tocqueville 1874 II, 245).

Tocqueville begins his examination of American institutions with a thorough overview of the geography, and Hunter (1995) notes that he portrays "the physical nature of the country [as] the primary force in shaping the new civilization" (157). Still, he plays down the impact of the landscape. Montesquieu and Rousseau were predominant figures among a tradition of scholars, who attributed a major significance of the geography to the appropriate form of government, but Tocqueville warns against exaggerations in this regard (Frängsmyr 2000; Rousseau 2001). However, this does not rule out that a future is inscribed in the landscape and it certainly does not rule out God. On the contrary, God's guidance will lead the new nation into the future and Tocqueville finds the evidence for that belief in the gorgeous landscape of Mississippi (Tocqueville 1874 I, 19, 30).

The temporal dimensions of the nation—past, present, future—are in different ways inscribed on the landscape in the travel narratives by Tocqueville, Martineau and Bremer. Nature and climate define the people and the landscape becomes the carrier of a history and a future. For Tocqueville, the landscape functions primarily as economic facts that will benefit the nation (as the valley of Mississippi) or as sensuous facts that will affect the morals in disastrous ways (as in Cuba). These preconditions, however, are created by God and thereby linked to the transcendental mission of the nation. For Martineau, the landscape is inscribed with the Indian nations' past; the present and future of the nation are understood in terms of natural laws working for the progress of mankind, which is mirrored by the novelty of the landscape.

Bremer attributes the broadest significance to the landscape: the nation's past is inscribed on the landscape and transforms it to a "poetic soil." The glorious vastness of the Western wilderness and the soothing air of Cuba will foster a nation of higher moral standing, if only the liberty that the landscape entices is checked by sound political institutions. The landscape is intimately connected to national characteristics. In fact, she believes that the landscape of Minnesota would provide a suitable environment for Scandinavian people precisely because she perceives the Nordic landscape to be duplicated in Minnesota: the lakes, the plains of Skåne, the valleys of Norrland, the rivers and high mountains of Norway and the coasts of Denmark are all present in this newly born state. Her conclusion is that Minnesota is the perfect land for a "*New Scandinavia*."[17] Bremer is trying to imagine a national past for the immigrants in the landscape, to create a connection that simply does not exist.

---

17 "rätt ett land för ett Nytt Skandinavien" (Bremer 1853a II, 350–51).

The landscape was part of these liberal thinkers' concept of the nation, but in the case of America, the landscape could only apply to the present and the future, since the nation consisted of different nationalities and the indigenous nationalities were exiled.

The People and the Nation

The tension between the revolutionary-democratic and the national concepts of the nation is most conspicuously played out regarding the people. The youth of the American nation is constantly evoked; for instance, Martineau writes that she regards "the American people as a great embryo poet" (Martineau 1837 I, 20). In Tocqueville's words, America was the opportunity to witness the birth of a nation, an event otherwise hidden in an obscured and distant past (Tocqueville 1874 I, 42, II, 192). Yet, the birth he had in mind was not the declaration of independence, but the American people beginning with the "the first Puritan who landed on those shores."[18] And when Bremer reflects on the youth of the American people, she specifies the age to two centuries instead of barely one—an "early morning" when it comes to nations (Bremer 1853b II, 151; "en morgonstund," Bremer 1853a II, 169). Obviously, the Constitution did not create the American people, according to Bremer, Tocqueville and Martineau: the people preceded the state. Still, the matter of how different nationalities will become one is a matter of vital importance that entices comprehensive discussions. Language, however, is not an issue.

The linguistic criterion for nationhood does not become central until the end of the nineteenth century (Hobsbawm 1990, 102). It did not play any part in the national movements in North and South America, and at the time of the French Revolution, some 50 percent of the Frenchmen actually did not even speak French (Anderson 1991, 67; Hobsbawm 1990, 60). Hobsbawm reminds us that national languages are "semi-artificial constructs": "They are the opposite of what nationalist mythology supposes them to be, namely the primordial foundations of national culture and the matrices of the national mind" (54). To the concept of the nation endorsed by Bremer, Tocqueville and Martineau, language was not a defining feature, but morals and manners certainly were.

The creation of a new people out of the various immigrating nations required a melting process. Martineau considers the different nationalities

---

18 Tocqueville 2006 I, ch. XVII part I; "le premier puritain qui aborda sur ses rivages" (Tocqueville 1874 II, 192).

as "elements" that will contribute to a higher "moral value" comparable to the country's "material wealth":

> There can scarcely be a finer set of elements for the composition of a nation than the United States now contain. It will take centuries to fuse them; and by that time, pride of ancestry,—vanity of physical deriva-tion,—will be at an end. The ancestry of moral qualities will be the only pedigree preserved; and of these every civilized nation under heaven possesses an ample, and probably an equal share. Let the United States then cherish their industrious Germans and Dutch; their hardy Irish; their intelligent Scotch; their kindly Africans, as well as the intellectual Yankee, the insouciant Southerner, and the complacent Westerner. All are good in their way; and augment the moral value of their country, as diversities of soil, climate, and productions, do its material wealth. (Mar-tineau 1837 I, 111)

She rejoices in the distinct characters of different nations, she returns on sev-eral occasions to examine their differences, and takes special care to separate the English, Scottish and Irish characters (Martineau 1837 II, 38). In fact, the writers' own respective national belonging becomes most clearly visible when singling out what European nationalities that need to be separated.

If Martineau distinguished between the different Great Britain nationali-ties, Bremer carefully characterized the different Scandinavian nationalities. It would have been especially important for her to distinguish between Swed-ish and Norwegian national characteristics, since as a friend to Stina Som-merhielm, the widow of the former Norwegian prime minister, she was keenly aware of the dissatisfaction in Norway regarding the union with Sweden (Haarder Ekman 2010, 146). Swedes like to enjoy themselves and to throw parties—an aspect of the national character that might bring disaster in the wilderness, as some failed Swedish settlements proved. Norwegian workers were definitely better settlers, according to Bremer. Swedes will bring beauty and merriness to America, but after visiting Swedish homes in the New World, she was happy to put her faith in the influence of the Anglo-Norman morals to teach the Swedes order and cleanliness (Bremer 1853a II, 262ff).

Bremer payed considerably less attention to the distinctions between other European nations, although she certainly acknowledged them and described the characteristics in much the same way as Martineau. The general spirit was a new combination of German transcendentalism, its "speculative thought," and Anglo-Norman "practical intuition," Bremers claimed, and the latter had the most profound influence (Bremer 1853b II,151; Bremer 1853a II, 169). For instance, "although two-thirds of the population of the Mississippi-valley consists of Scandinavians, Germans, Irish, and French, yet they are governed by the legislative and formative spirit of the Anglo-Norman."[19] In this respect, she followed Tocqueville's argument.

Tocqueville basically ignored all other European nationalities apart from the Anglo-Saxons. He even claimed that he could hardly imagine that America was actually separated from Britain (Tocqueville 1874 III, 58). Everything hinges on morals and manners: "manners are the only durable and resisting power in a people."[20] The morals of the American people were, according to Tocqueville, a legacy from the puritans of New England and as they constantly moved out to all corners of the country, their morals would eventually permeate the whole population (Tocqueville 1874 I: 42ff, 54ff, II, 382, 416–17).

Morals and manners define the nation, and the consequences for Tocqueville are that the concept of the nation could apply to different strata of the population. The American union of states was a federation of several nations. For Tocqueville, a lawyer and a politician whose point of departure for the examination of the U.S. was the social order and the legislation, it was important to stress that each state is a nation—they have not lost their different nationalities (Tocqueville 1874 I, 93, II, 352). The federal government was explicitly not national (Tocqueville 1874 I, 205). On the other hand, since he attributed a strong formative power to the law, he did recognize that in relation to the federal government and to the Constitution, the American people did after all constitute a nation (Tocqueville 1874 I, 196ff, 234–35, II, 361, 391). The issue is even more complicated by the fact that he considered large parties with opposing material interests within a nation—such as the South and the North states disagreement over tariff legislation—to constitute different nation. Indeed, associations within the parties or different social classes, or even the army, may be considered as nations within the nation ("une nation à part dans la nation," Tocqueville 1874 II, 4ff, 33–33, 111, III, 437). In a democracy, Tocqueville claimed, even each new generation should be considered to be a new people (Tocqueville 1874 III, 95).

---

19 Bremer 1853b II, 395. "[...] ehuru två tredjedelar af Missisippidalens folkmängd består af skandinaver och tyskar, irländare och fransmän, så är dock den laggifvande och bildande anden, den anglo-normanska" (Bremer 1853a II, 440).

20 Tocqueville 2006 I: ch. XVI part II; "les mœurs forment la seule puissance résistante et durable chez un peuple" (Tocqueville 1874 II, 182).

It is obvious that Tocqueville does not use the nation in a prescriptive sense, but rather as an investigative tool to analyse different kinds of communities that may on the one hand create a sense of belonging and, on the other hand, may create tensions in the wider community. Like Bremer, when she refuses to decide whether the nation refers to a province, to the territory currently defined as the kingdom of Sweden or to Scandinavia without agreed-on borders, he studies the bonds that will keep a nation together. The bonds that posed the greatest threat for the American nation were, according to all three writers, the bonds of slavery.

Bremer, Tocqueville and Martineau all rejected slavery. However, they still believed in distinct characteristics of different races—though Bremer confessed that she could hardly see the difference between mulattos and Spanish in Cuba (Bremer 1854a III, 128). The origin of races was a highly debated issue during the eighteenth century (Frängsmyr 2000, 69–70). The number of races could vary (72–73). Tocqueville and Bremer both refer to European authorities when they recognize three different races, in Bremer's words: "People of the Day—the Whites; People of the Night—the Negroes; and People of the Twilight—the Indians of the Eastern and Western hemispheres."[21]

In Cuba, Bremer came in contact with newly arrived slaves from Africa. The slave-ships disgusted her, but she took the opportunity to compare the people who had grown up in Africa with the black people who had grown up in the U.S. Most importantly, this provided her with the opportunity to distinguish between different African "nations." The Gangas, the Luccomées, the Mandingos and the Callavalis (or Caraballis) are all described as to their differences in appearance, such as features and tattoos, and customs such as their manner of dancing (Bremer 1854a III, 133–34, 252ff). She also acknowledged social ranks among African peoples and the impact on the behaviour in the slave community. American blacks had lost their "native" nationality and had become, as Tocqueville puts it, isolated between two peoples.[22] Bremer found this deplorable, and she found comfort in the awakening of a national consciousness she perceived as emergent among a sector of black preachers (Bremer 1853a I, 450, II, 464ff).

The worship of blacks was a revelation to Bremer—she enjoyed the services and especially the singing; she considered black music to be the truly original folksongs of the New World, comparing their peculiarities to the peculiarities

---

21 Bremer 1853b II, 311. "[...] dagfolk (de hvita), nattfolk (negrerna) och skymningsfolk (Indianerna i östra och vestra verldsdelarne" (Bremer 1853a II, 348).

22 "il est resté isolé entre les deux peuples" (Tocqueville 1874 II, 262).

of Scandinavian folksongs (Bremer 1853a II, 410, 1854a III, 46). Her ideas of
the characteristics of blacks were much the same as those that would form
the eugenic discourse at the turn of the century 1900. However, for Bremer
these characteristics created excellent conditions for a peculiar and nourish-
ing worship of God. For her, this was a crucial requirement for belonging to
the future nation. As Hobsbawm (1990) points out, for many liberals during
the nineteenth century, the nation was only a stage of evolution, "second-best
to world unity" (31, 38–39).

The Mission of the Nation
America had a vital part in God's plan for humankind—that conviction
united Bremer, Tocqueville, Martineau and many of their contemporaries.
America's special mission was, in Bremer's words, to perform "the emancipation of humanity socially and politically."[23] In Tocqueville'e explanation, the
mission is due to the expanding drive of the white race and God's plan to
create a fantastic land where the principle of democracy could be planted
(Tocqueville 1874 I, 19, 30). America is God's gift to protect liberty "as if it
had been kept in reserve by the Deity."[24] Democracy will bring nations nearer
to each other until the entire humanity forms a democracy, Tocqueville predicted. This will bring out the true face of humanity and God's plan will
finally appear (Tocqueville 1874 III, 122–23).

For Bremer, another condition was more determining: the multiplicity of
religious communities. All of these communities had suffered persecution
and exile for their faith, the result of which is a sharpened call of the "inner
voice" and resolve. This shared experience had strengthened the morals of
the nations, and made them fit to conquer the New World and unite in high
religious morals (Bremer 1853a I, 219ff, 1854a III, 511ff). The future of the
American nation, in Martineau's account on the other hand, was to bring
out the idea that possessed "the Americans from their first day of national
existence till now." The evolution of this idea was certain even if it might not
always look that way: "whenever the time shall arrive, which cannot but arrive,
when the nation shall be so fully possessed of the complete idea as by moral
necessity to act it out, they will be as far superior to nations which act upon
the experience and expediency of their time as the great poet is superior to

---

23 Bremer 1853b II, 409. "[...] menniskans sociala och politiska frigörelse" (Bremer 1853a II, 455).

24 Tocqueville 2006 I, ch. XVII part I; "comme si Dieu l'eût tenue en réserve" (Tocqueville 1874 II, 194).

common men" (Martineau 1837 I, 21). The nation has a transcendent purpose that will appear in time.

As noted earlier, the idea of utopia was connected to America from the
start. This was a connection that was reinforced as the Pilgrim Fathers linked
the colony to New Testament eschatology. This Christian dimension of time
and its American application is of crucial importance to Bremer's analysis of
the U.S. Lauren Berlant (1991) draws attention to the representation of time
in her study of Nathaniel Hawthorne, *The Anatomy of National Fantasy*. His
novel *The Scarlet Letter* (1850) is set in Massachusetts in the seventeenth century and foregrounds the idea of utopia. She argues that the American utopia
in Hawthorne's account is related to

> Puritan and post-Revolutionary War political cultures, both of which
> used the promise of millennial and secular collective perfectibility to cre-
> ate a sphere of projected political experience and knowledge that com-
> peted with and even sublated the pressure of material political realities.
> (Berlant 1991, 7)

The utopian promise to the individual to be transformed into a citizen—that
is, to be part of a large totality—is indeed the promise of any modern nation,
but this is especially true of the U.S., since the Puritans placed the New World
"within the time frame of God's providential 'calendar'," as Berlant puts it (25,
97).

After visiting the West, Bremer abandoned the idea of utopia, the new paradise, but not the idea of America as "the promised land," the land of the
future. Its mission is now framed in another Biblical trope, namely the end
of history: "we must not expect a Utopia from America, but rather a day of
judgment."[25] The Dooms-day will force the people to choose between light-
ness and darkness, and decide the fate of humankind. Slavery complicated
the future and she had become overwhelmed by the movement, the haste of
the New World: "The life of North America exhibits such a hurrying onward,
such a concentration of the fullness [sic] of development in good and evil."[26]
The political vision of a promised land, joining all people in brotherhood,
seems to be a hopeful and loving prediction of the development of the notion

---

25 Bremer 1853b III, 458. "...af denna verldsbildning är icke ett *Utopien*, utan – *en domedag*" (Bremer
1853a II, 442, 1854a III, 520).

26 Bremer 1853b III, 458. "Norra Amerikas lif häntyder på ett sådant framskyndande, en sådan
koncentration af utvecklingens fullhet i godt och – i ondt." (Bremer 1854a III, 520).

of the nation. However, Bremer recognized only one Father to hold the brotherhood together, and this will in her view have dire consequences for some nations.

Bremer's views on the Indians was no doubt influenced by her contact with white Americans. However, it was a harsh view even for her own times. She reacted in particular to the treatment of women: they "are evidently merely their husbands' beasts of burden" (Bremer 1853b II, 284; "männernas lastdjur," Bremer 1853a II, 319). Martineau also noticed this with contempt (Martineau 1837 I, 147–48), but she still appreciated "the good faith, and other virtues" of the Indians (Martineau 1837 I, 182). Bremer rejected even the Indian dignity, claiming that all the Indian virtues had a root in pride: "The virtue of the Indian is selfish."[27] Her final judgement is that she "cannot possibly wish for a prolonged existence to that people, who reckon cruelty among their virtues, and who reduce the weak to beasts of burden."[28]

Martineau reacted vehemently against the abuse of Indians and Indian territory (Martineau 1837 I, 169–70) and mistrusted the missionaries since they tended to "take from the savage the venerable and the true which he possessed, and to force upon him something else which is to him neither venerable nor true" (Martineau 1837 I, 196). Bremer drew a completely different conclusion: the Indians were not susceptible to higher education of the soul and could not adopt the Christian truths (Bremer 1853a II, 345). Therefore, they were doomed to extinction under the invasion of a "nobler and more humane people" (Bremer 1853b II, 311; "ädlare och menskligare," Bremer 1853a II, 347–48). Even so, there is little reason to over-emphasise the difference between Bremer and Martineau; a hierarchy from savage to higher levels of culture was essential even to Martineau (for example Martineau 1837 II, 103). Tocqueville ended up with much the same conclusion, but from a slightly different angle: his argument was not grounded in the Indians susceptibility to religion, but in their inferiority as a race. His elaborate descriptions of the various causes for the disastrous situation are sympathetic to the Indian nations, but their passions, their vices and savage virtues have sentenced them to destruction. His final statement was that the Indians were only in America in waiting for another race to take over the land. The

---

27 Bremer 1853b II: 307. "Indianens dygd är sjelfvisk" (Bremer 1853a II, 347).

28 Bremer 1853b II: 311. "[...] så kan jag omöjligt önska långt lif åt folk, som räknar grymhet bland sina dygder, och gör den svaga till lastdjur" (Bremer 1853a II, 347).

New World "seemed to be prepared to be the abode of a great nation, yet unborn."[29]

The Bonds of the Nation

Bremer's, Tocqueville's and Martineau's respective concepts of the nation cannot be contained by either the categories of revolutionary-democratic or nationalism. The American nation *did* exist prior to the state, according to them, and *yet* is still in the making. They studied the U.S. *because* of the revolutionary-democratic origin of the nation, but made sense of their findings within a nationalist paradigm. Their concepts of the nation share the same elements, but differ as to what aspects are accentuated. Tocqueville expected that the democratic nation would be expressed in new literary forms and styles, and believed that the glorious landscape was evidence that America was God's gift to liberty, which would make the true face of the mankind appear. To Martineau, the landscape was inscribed by indigenous history. However, the future mission of the American nation was to bring out the idea of freedom in accordance with natural law—this was what the future national literature would give expression to in a way already carried out by the legislation. An even heavier weight is attributed to the landscape in Bremer's account. She imagined a national past in the American landscape for immigrants and awaited a national literature that would become the literary expression of the vast wilderness. The Biblical imagery in her descriptions should be understood literally: it suggests the Christian mission of the American nation. Differences between the means for achieving the goal are explained by how they picture the bonds of society.

Morals and manners defined the nation for these early nineteenth-century thinkers precisely because they are the most obvious social bonds, but that does not explain how these bonds are knitted. Martineau described democracy as a special kind of bonds. The Constitution declares the "law of universal justice" to be the founding principle; a democracy makes every citizen "bound together by equal political obligation" (Martineau 1837 I, 4). Every man, she explains,

> may be regarded [under two aspects]: as a solitary being, with inherent powers, and an omnipotent will [...]; and again, as a being infinitely con-

---

29 Tocqueville 2006 I: ch. I; "ils n'étaient là, en quelque sorte, qu'*en attendant*"; "le berceau vide d'une grande nation" (Tocqueville 1874 I, 39).

nected with all other beings, with none but derived powers, with a heav-
enly-directed will; a creature, a subject, a transparent medium through
which the workings of principles are to be eternally revealed. (Martineau
1837 II, 64)

The Old World favoured the first aspect, but in the New World the connection
between all individuals—what Martineau calls the "sublimer" aspect of man-
hood—will be more and more apparent. In her view, democracy entices "rev-
erencing instead of appropriating the privileges of other wards of Providence"
(Martineau 1837 II, 64). Martineau stresses that oppressive bonds destroy the
individual and insists that oppressed people may appear as animals. However,
this is explained by how they are treated by their fellow humans. The logic,
in her view, is simple: a person, who is treated as a human being, will act like
one (Martineau 1837 I, 99ff, 150). While Martineau believed that Christianity is "the root of all democracy" (Martineau 1837 II, 217), she clearly gave
precedence to the political implications of being "infinitely connected with
all other beings" when it came to defining the nation. She rejoiced in the
multitude of manners, but in her view, manners and morals depended on how
individuals were treated by each other, and ultimately on the political institutions and the legislation.

Tocqueville agreed that the hierarchic bonds of aristocracy served to keep
people in obedience, but the solution must not be a loosening of the "health-
bringing bonds of discipline" of the individual ("les liens salutaires de la
discipline," Tocqueville 1874 II, 142, III, 146). The object of the nation is
to bring the social bonds of the law in harmony with the natural bonds of
opinions, taste and faith, that is with *les mœurs* (Tocqueville 1874 I, 16). The
social bonds may weaken for inner reasons, such as natural bonds growing
stronger. Tocqueville feared that democracy would have such an effect, as I
mentioned earlier. However, social bonds might also weaken because of exterior reasons, such as violence to the community. When the social bonds dissolved, the nation ceased to exist, Tocqueville explained, as was the case with
many Indian nations (Tocqueville 1874 II, 274). He emphasised the political
institutions and the legislation, but since the success of social order ultimately
is to be found in the manners and morals, which in their turn rely on the
disciplinary bonds of the individual, the social bonds of the nation were ultimately a question of individual discipline.

To Bremer, the most important bonds were the natural bonds in a meta-

phoric sense: the nations are siblings, relating to one Father, and this transcendental bond takes precedence over all other bonds, or rather, it guarantees the validity of all other bonds.

> And in the attainment of the most important object in the solution of
> the highest problem of humanity—a fraternal people, I believe that the
> Father of all people laid his hand upon the head of his youngest son, as
> our Charles the Ninth did, saying, "He shall do it! he shall do it!"[30]

Bremer went to America in search for "the *New Man* and his world; the new
humanity and the sight of its future on the soil of the New World" (Bremer
1853b II, 381). The New Man was the gathering of all people in a new nation,
or indeed a new race, as part of God's evolution of humankind. It appears to
be a vision of inclusion, but it is as much a vision of exclusion: only Christian
nations will be part of the future and be able to contribute with their national
characteristics to the New Man. The bonds connect the nations and every
citizen to God. The siblings do therefore not relate directly to each other, but
are united only through God.

Regardless of whether the bonds of society were knitted by the Constitution,
by the individual's adherence to morals and manners or by the family of God,
"the nation" in these mid-nineteenth century liberal studies of America was a
conceptual tool. This tool was used in order to analyse modern, democratic
society. The familiarity of the term should not fool us: the content of "the
nation" in these accounts is foreign to our own usage. According to Bremer,
Tocqueville and Martineau, the nation had first and foremost a transcendental purpose: the bonds of society tied the nation to an evolutionary mission.

---

30 Bremer 1853b I, 254. "Och för lösningen af mensklighetens största problem och högsta mål –
skapandet af *ett brödrafolk*, tror jag att folkens Fader lagt sin hand på yngsta sonens hufvud, sågande
(som vår konung Carl IX): '*han* skall göra't!'" (Bremer 1853a I, 290).

References

Anderson, B. 1991. *Imagined Communities: Reflections on the Origin and Spread of Nationalism.* London & New York: Verso.

Berlant, L. 1991. *The Anatomy of National Fantasy: Hawthorne, Utopia, and Everyday Life.* Chicago and London: University of Chicago Press.

Bohlin, A. 2008. *Röstens anatomi. Läsningar av politik i Elin Wägners Silverforsen, Selma Lagerlöfs Löwensköldtrilogi och Klara Johansons Tidevarvskåserier.* Umeå: Bokförlaget h:ström.

Bohlin, A. 2013. "Den manliga frimodigheten: Gud och andra män hos Fredrika Bremer." In *Kvinnorna gör mannen: Maskulinitetskonstruktioner i kvinnors text och bild 1500–2000.* Edited by Fjelkestam, K., H. Hilland, and D. Tjeder, 311– 342. Göteborg and Stockholm: Makadam.

Bremer, F. 1834. *Nya teckningar utur hvardagslifvet: Presidentens döttrar, berättelse af en guvernant.* Stockholm: L. J. Hjerta.

———. 1853–1854a. *Hemmen i den Nya Verlden: En dagbok i bref, skrifna under tvenne års resor i Norra Amerika och på Cuba.* Vol. I–III. Stockholm: P. A. Norstedt & söner.

———. 1853b. *The Homes of the New World: Impressions of America.* Vol. I–III. Translated by Mary Howitt. London: Arthur Hall, Virtue, & Co.

———. 1916 *Fredrika Bremers brev, del II 1838–1846.* Edited by K. Johanson and E. Kleman. Stockholm: P. A. Norstedt & söners förlag.

Bremer, F. 1996. *Brev: Ny följd II 1853–1865.* Edited by C. Burman. Hedemora: Gidlunds Förlag.

Burman, C. 2001. *Bremer: En biografi.* Stockholm: Albert Bonniers Förlag.

Frängsmyr, C. 2000. *Klimat och karaktär: Naturen och människan i sent svenskt 1700-tal.* Stockholm: Natur & Kultur.

Haarder Ekman, K. 2010. *"Mitt hems gränser vidgades": En studie i den kulturella skandinavismen under 1800-talet.* Göteborg and Stockholm: Makadam förlag.

Harper, L. M. 2001. *Solitary Travelers: Nineteenth-Century Women's Travel Narratives and the Scientific Vocation.* Cranbury, London and Ontario: Associated University Press.

Hobsbawm, E. J. 1990. *Nations and Nationalism since 1780: Programme, Myth, Reality.* Cambridge and New York: Cambridge University Press.

Hunter, S. 1995. *Harriet Martineau: The Poetics of Moralism.* Aldershot and Brookfield: Scholar Press.

Kahan, A. S. 1992. *Aristocratic Liberalism. The Social and Political Thought of Jacob Burckhardt, John Stuart Mill, and Alexis de Tocqueville.* Oxford and New York: Oxford University Press.

Kleman, E. 1938. *Fredrika Bremer and America*. Stockholm: Åhlén & Åkerlund.

Lagerkvist, A. 2005. *Amerikafantasier: Kön, medier och visualitet i svenska reseskildringar från USA 1945–63*. Stockholm: Institutionen för Journalistik, medier och kommunikation, Stockholms universitet.

Lofsvold, L. A. 1999. *Fredrika Bremer and the Writing of America*. Lund: Lund University Press.

Manns, U. 2001. "Fredrika Bremer: kvinnorörelsens galjonsfigur." In *Mig törstar! Studier i Fredrika Bremers spår*, edited by Å. Arping and B. Ahlmo-Nilsson, 259–75. Hedemora: Gidlunds.

Martineau, H. 1837. *Society in America*. Vol I–II Paris: Baudry's European Library.

McKeon, M. 1987. *The Origins of the English Novel 1600–1740*. Baltimore and London: The Johns Hopkins University Press.

Poovey, M. 2008. *Genres of the Credit Economy: Mediating Value in Eighteenth- and Nineteenth-Century Britain*. Chicago and London: University of Chicago Press.

Pratt, M. L. 1992. *Imperial Eyes: Travel Writing and Transculturation*. London and New York: Routledge.

Qvist, G. 1969. *Fredrika Bremer och kvinnans emancipation: Opinionshistoriska studier*. Kvinnohistoriskt arkiv 8 Göteborg: Akademiförlaget.

Rousseau, J.-J. 2001. *Du contrat social* [1762]. Edited by B. Bernardi. Paris: Flammarion.

Runeby, N. 1969. *Den nya världen och den gamla: Amerikabild och emigrationsuppfattning i Sverige 1820–1860*. Studia historica Upsaliensia XXX, Uppsala: Svenska bokförlaget.

Stenqvist, G., and G. Furuland. 2009. "Fredrika Bremer i Sverige och Finland." *Biblis* 46: 56–62.

Thompson, C. 2011. *Travel Writing*. London and New York: Routledge.

de Tocqueville, A. 1874. *De la démocratie en Amérique*. Vol. I–III [1835–1840], Œuvres completes nouvelle edition. Paris: Michel Lévy frères.

———. 2006. *Democracy In America*. Vol. I–II. Translated by Henry Reeve. The project Gutenberg E-Book.

Wendelius, L. 1985. *Fredrika Bremers Amerikabild: En studie i Hemmen i den Nya Verlden*. Skrifter utgivna av Svenska Litteratursällskapet 39 Stockholm: Almqvist & Wiksell International.

Selma Lagerlöf, Narrative and Counter-Narrative
The Question of Sources in the Historical Understanding of an Author's Works

*Jenny Bergenmar**

Abstract

When writing the history of an author's oeuvre, canonical and public sources are given precedence. The professional readers' (critics') statements about what is considered the major work of the author are central in this historiography, while letters to the author from the audience, reports in newspapers or magazines about the author's public appearances or autobiographical accounts of the author are usually left out. In this article the case of Selma Lagerlöf is explored through more peripheral sources: letters, (auto)biographical accounts, reports from different events in women's magazines and some "minor" texts in her oeuvre. What links between public and private events and texts appear when these neglected sources are placed in the centre of the analysis, and how does this change the narrative of the author's reception and significance? I will focus on the question of women's rights and conditions in society, revealing themselves to be important both in Lagerlöf's "minor" texts and in the reception of her works, and discuss how Fredrika Bremer's legacy is visible in Lagerlöf's life and writing—specifically through the question of women's citizenship and education as well as women's role as educators. Only by putting the different sources side by side do the links between history, autobiography and fiction appear, making cultural memories visible and, at the same time, re-evaluating canonical truths.

Introduction

The literary history of Selma Lagerlöf's oeuvre—or any author's oeuvre—is mainly comprised of canonical sources: the position within the literary establishment (and not its social functions outside of it), the texts considered to be of the greatest aesthetic value (and not the ones written for

* Jenny Bergenmar is Senior Lecturer in Comparative Literature an the Department of Literature, History of Ideas and Religion at the University of Gothenburg

specific purposes or occasions). There is a predominant story about Lagerlöf's oeuvre, stemming from some contemporary critics, such as Oscar Lev-
ertin, which was later transferred to literary handbooks (Nordlund 2005).
In this story, Selma Lagerlöf is cast as a storyteller, closely connected with
tradition (rather than modernity), with fantasy (rather than reality) and
with timeless wisdom (rather than political consciousness). The Swedish
Academy's award ceremony speech in 1909, presented by Claes Annerstedt,
exemplifies this tendency. It foregrounds the author as storyteller, "eliciting
beautiful secrets from fairy tales, living folk legends, and saints' stories;
secrets that had been hidden from the worldly-wise but which true simplicity perceives" (Annerstedt 1909). In Annerstedt's speech Selma Lagerlöf is
explicitly made a feminine author, disconnected from modernity and its
political issues, such as women's suffrage. She is presented as the opposite
of a conscious and elaborate artist, the keywords instead being simplicity,
tradition and spirituality.

Looking at the sources comprising this story, we find Lagerlöf's literary
works, while her non-literary texts pass unmentioned. The canonical novels
of her oeuvre, such as *The Story of Gösta Berling* (1891), *Jerusalem* (1901–1902),
The Emperor of Portugallia (1914) and *Charlotte Löwensköld* (1925) fit into this
narrative, although they may well be interpreted as both political and modern. Research on Selma Lagerlöf during the last 10–15 years has to a large
extent been devoted to challenging the image of Selma Lagerlöf as a "traditional" storyteller, in reading her works as modern(ist), experimental, aesthetic and innovative from different perspectives (Karlsson 2002; Bergenmar 2003; Nordlund 2005; Thorup-Thomsen 2007; Wijkmark 2009). Some
have also read Lagerlöf in an explicitly feminist social context (Stenberg
2002; Bohlin 2008). Even though these studies all have contributed to revis-
ing the image of her oeuvre, to a varying extent they share the tendency
within literary history to reread and reinterpret the literary texts, especially
the great, canonized ones, or their reception within the literary establishment.[1]

In historical studies and cultural studies Selma Lagerlöf's oeuvre has been

---

1 There are a few exceptions to this tendency in the titles mentioned—Stenberg uses biography
and Lagerlöf's early, unpublished poetry, Thorup Thomsen adds an interesting discussion about
some marginalized texts in Lagerlöf's oeuvre ("Värmländsk naturskönhet," "På strandpromenaden"
and "Vädjan till Amerika") to his main discussion about *The Adventures of Nils Holgersson*, Wijkmark
concentrates on six short stories instead of Lagerlöf's novels. Bohlin discusses Lagerlöf's engagement
in the contemporary political and feminist issues, but she mainly stays within the framework of
Lagerlöf's novels and her well-known speech "Home and State."

researched within a different theoretical framework. Here other sources than
the literary texts are used; for example, contemporary media and documents
from the archives of organizations or individual persons. Lagerlöf's public
appearances—i.e. how she performs her oeuvre in public—are in focus, as
well as the reception of these appearances (Petersens 2006; Pipping and Olsson 2010). The public aspects of Lagerlöf's author identity are highlighted
in the research on her literary texts and on her public appearances. But the
surge of research on Lagerlöf during the last ten years has also produced
some biographies and letter editions, providing perspectives on the complex interplay between the public and the private, and showing how Lagerlöf
manoeuvred strategically between those spheres (Edström 2003; Toijer-Nilsson 2006; Englund and Kåreland 2008; Carlsson 2009, 2010). Reception studies and the closely related areas of the history of reading and the history of
the book are research fields which can potentially combine different sources
to contribute to the understanding of the historical use and significance of
authors and their texts. Robert Darnton underlines this in his seminal essay
"First Steps towards a History of Reading": "fiction could be fleshed out and
compared with documents—actual suicide notes, diaries, and letters to the
editor" (Darnton 1986). Literature is a source for cultural history among others, and not completely intelligible without other sources.

In this article I aim to develop the analysis of the interplay between the
private, public and semi-public in the understanding of an oeuvre, through a
combined analysis of literary, biographical/autobiographical texts and reception documents. These different types of texts—letters, biography, fiction,
documented memories, reports in magazines—can be considered as parts
of the Selma Lagerlöf "archive." The concept of "archive" has been used as
a means to include fiction as a source of historical knowledge (for an overview, see Pascoe 2004), not least in queer studies (Cvetkovich 2009; Danbolt,
Rowley, and Wolters 2009), but it can also be used to discover what voices
are silenced in the narrating of an oeuvre. Following Michel Foucault, the
archive is a "system of discursivity" (Foucault 1972, 129)—what is present in
the archive is defined by what is absent. Foucault's focus on exclusions from
the archive points to the question of power relations governing our conceptualizations of the past. Evidently, the sources considered in this article are
not absent from the archive, but silenced under the canonical discourse.
What links between public and private events and texts appear when these
neglected sources are placed in the centre of the analysis and how does this
change the narrative of an oeuvre?

Autobiography, Biography and the Narration of an Authorship

Selma Lagerlöf's lifetime (1858–1940) coincided with important changes for
women in modern society. Turning to the reception of her works in the audience's letters to her and the reports on her public appearances, the question
of women's citizenship appears to be central. This is also true for some of
the "minor" texts of Lagerlöf's authorship: "Mamsell Fredrika" (1891), "Two
Prophecies" (1908) and "Home for Aged Schoolmistresses: A Call for Fundraising" (1912). They are all more or less literary texts. However, they will also
be read as political statements. I will discuss these in relation to Lagerlöf's
well-known speech at the Sixth Convention of the International Women's Suffrage Alliance in Stockholm in 1911, "Home and State," but above all focus on
the responses to it.[2] The genres I use span from speech and newspaper articles to short stories. Two of them have explicit political purposes ("Home and
State" and "Home for Aged Schoolmistresses: A Call for Fundraising"), two of
them have biographical or autobiographical aspects ("Mamsell Fredrika" and
"Two Prophecies"). At the same time, they are all stories, and the narrative
quality may make them less viable—or in some historians' opinion—less valid
as historical sources, for example compared to a regular political pamphlet.

Both fiction and autobiography are problematic sources for the historian,
being individual rather than collective, subjective rather than objective and to
a varying degree fictional rather than factual (Iddeng 2005; Bagerius 2011).[3]
"For historians, taking autobiographical writing seriously means acknowledging an alternative approach to narrating the past, one that cannot simply be
dismissed as fiction," as the historian Jeremy Popkin writes (2005, 13). Letters can be more or less autobiographical, and are characterized by the same
ambiguous position as an historical source. Letters are not simply sources
where documentation of persons and events can be retrieved, or pieces of life
writing, they can also be seen as literary texts, "a representation that has to
be explored in context with the signatory, addressee, and the society" (Halldórsdóttir 2013; see also Stanley 2004, 212). In the case of Lagerlöf, the letters
highlight the use and reception of the texts. What might be called anecdotal historical evidence, such as memories or reports of meetings with Selma
Lagerlöf on different occasions, are also valuable sources for understanding

---

2 Of these texts only "Mamsell Fredrika" and "Home and State" are available in translation.
These will be used, in all other cases the translations are my own. The titles in Swedish: "Mamsell
Fredrika," "Två spådomar," "Hem och stat," "Åldersdomshem för svenska lärarinnor: Ett upprop om
penningeinsamling."

3 See also Katarina Leppänen's article in this issue.

the social context of the oeuvre. In contrast to these, Elin Wägner's biography is more of a master narrative of the oeuvre, but since it also builds on personal encounters with the author, it does not escape autobiographical features.

Narrating an Author Identity

When she published her first novel, *The Story of Gösta Berling* (1891), and the following collection of short stories, *Invisible Links* (1894) Lagerlöf was employed as a teacher in the town of Landskrona in the south of Sweden. She was born in a middle-class family in Värmland in 1858, as the fifth child of Lieutenant Lagerlöf and his wife Louise. From her birth she suffered from a hip injury, which, in her biographical writings *Mårbacka* (1922), *Memories of My Childhood* (1930) and *The Diary of Selma Lagerlöf* (1932), is an important element in the narrative of herself as an author in the making. Elin Wägner remarks that she used her disability to escape from the conventional rules of the upbringing of girls (Wägner 1942, 36). In 1880, when Selma Lagerlöf was twenty-one, she met Eva Fryxell, a well-known figure in the women's movement. Fryxell encouraged Lagerlöf to get an education, but her father proved to be difficult to convince. Wägner effectively contrasts Lagerlöf's limited options with the horizons lying before some of her male countrymen: "At the same age as Heidenstam departed for his first honeymoon, and Nansen made his first polar expedition and Strindberg wrote *Mäster Olof*, Selma Lagerlöf entered the seminar" (Wägner 1942, 77, my translation). The seminar in question was the first institution for higher education of women in Sweden, Högre lärarin-neseminariet in Stockholm, opened in 1861 (Ullman 2004, 33).

Lagerlöf describes her fears when waiting for approval or rejection of her application to the seminar in the story "Two Prophecies" (1908, later included in the collection *Troll och människor* 1915). The exams had lasted almost a week and Selma Lagerlöf makes her young self into somewhat of a fighter. She enjoys the contest and feels quite confident about her achievement, even if her education by a governess at home in the province of Värmland might have been less solid than the others, who "have attended proper schools in cities" (Lagerlöf 1915, 223). What really causes her anguish is the prospect of her life if not admitted to the seminar. "If I fail now, I am finished. I will have to apply for a place as a governess with a salary of a few hundred crowns, or I will have to go back home and take care of the household" (Lagerlöf 1915, 224). Life as a spinster is her greatest fear, not because she regrets not being married and having children, but because she wants to be independent. When she finally gets the message that she had passed the exams, she releases her relief: "I am no longer helpless and dependent. I have a course open to me. I will earn my own living and control my own actions. It will be up to me to reach my own goals" (Lagerlöf 1915, 228). Education is in this case presented as the only escape from female confinement.

When Selma Lagerlöf, as an established author with a successful career, tells the story of herself as a twenty-three year old in "Two Prophecies," she contrasts the life of the working woman, with her own money, goals and independence, to the life of the unmarried woman confined to domestic life—the governess or the old maid still living in her parental home. Interestingly, this is not the beginning of the tale. Lagerlöf instead departs from the very start—her own birth in 1858. In the opening of the story, she gives two older women—her grandmother, the old Mrs Lagerlöf, and another relative, referred to as Aunt Wennervik—leading parts. Together they represent an impressive amount of women's experience. The old Mrs Lagerlöf has lived all her life in the room behind the kitchen, as a girl, as a married woman, as a widow and grandmother. She is always calm, has white hair and knits socks for her grandchildren. Aunt Wennervik is a clergyman's wife. People come to her for help, and she is prepared for any eventuality. She has been a housekeeper at many country houses, and knows everything from cooking wedding dinners and complicated weaving techniques to curing the sick and turning peasant daughters into good housewives. They are drinking coffee, knitting and speaking of what will become of the newborn child. When Aunt Wennervik tells the child's fortune with her deck of cards, it turns out that that the child will become something entirely different from her older female relatives: she will travel and live in different places, she will be hopeless at weaving and needlework, she will work with books and paperwork, she will not be healthy and she will never be married. The old Mrs Lagerlöf is obviously concerned. She interprets the prediction within the limited options of women at her time and, although she tries to see the possibilities even with these drawbacks, she is disappointed that the granddaughter will never be married.

In the telling of her making as a woman author, the questions of marriage, money and education are clearly important. Discussing the matter of marriage, Selma Lagerlöf uses the prophecy of sickness—namely, the problem with her hip joint that caused a limp, which she suffered from all her life. In her fictionalized diary, *The Diary of Selma Lagerlöf*, she makes her teenage self satisfied that the limp makes her unfit to marry as in this way she gains freedom to choose the path of the author (Lagerlöf 1932). Despite the obvious warmth and admiration in the description of the older relatives with their traditional female roles, there is also a clear indication that the prophecy tells something about a new world and new options for women in society. My point in discussing these examples is that the role of the spinster and the role of the author seem intricately connected in Selma Lagerlöf's own story of becoming an author. The spinster represents a waste of women, denied access to the public realm. At the same time, avoiding marriage seems a prerequisite for becoming an author.

Narrating Fredrika Bremer's Legacy

The connection between spinsterhood and being an author is also foregrounded in Selma Lagerlöf's short story "Mamsell Fredrika." It was first printed in 1891 in *Dagny: Journal For Social and Literary Interests*, one of the most important women's magazines at the time. Sophie Adlersparre, director of the Fredrika Bremer Association, the largest women's association in Sweden, was also editor of *Dagny*, which functioned as an organ for the Fredrika Bremer Association. Issue 1–2 1891 was a special edition, honouring Fredrika Bremer (1801–1865) twenty-five years after her death.[4] In the introduction, Sophie Adlersparre stresses her engagement in the women who seemed to lose their entire value as human beings when failing, or not wanting, to be married. According to Adlersparre it was the social theorist Harriet Martineau who made Bremer realize that the rights of women as citizens must begin in a reformation of the law. She claims that Bremer also came to embrace Martineau's conviction that women should be allowed to contribute to society through work in the public sphere. Work and education are Bremer's designated ways to counteract the waste of women in a society only considering their value as wives. "Should not every woman be educated so she can live and work independently, regardless of marriage?" Bremer asks (Adlersparre 1891, 14).[5]

Selma Lagerlöf's story "Mamsell Fredrika" continues on the same theme. Selma Lagerlöf addresses Fredrika Bremer not only as a fellow woman author, but also as an unmarried woman, a "mamsell." The story is at once a gender-political statement and a meta-commentary, in the shape of a ghost story. Considered in relation to Selma Lagerlöf's autobiographical accounts, the

---

4 All issues of *Dagny* are indexed and available in digital facsimiles at KvinnSam, National Resource Library for Gender Studies, Gothenburg University Library, and used as a source in this article, see http://www.ub.gu.se/kvinn/digtid/

5 Adlersparre is citing a letter from Bremer to her friend Brinkman.

story closely resembles a personal act of gratitude from the young woman who dared challenge the word of her father and leave home to be educated. "She has stirred young girls towards the wide activities of life," Lagerlöf writes (Lagerlöf [1894] 1899, 153) and Selma Lagerlöf presents herself as one of those girls.

The history of the seminar Lagerlöf attended, as well as the story of Bremer that Lagerlöf tells in "Mamsell Fredrika," is connected to Bremer's influential and much-debated novel *Hertha*. The novel was published in 1856 and provided a sharp criticism of the exclusion of women from educational institutions. It has been read as a feminist manifesto, and is credited as a contributing factor in the parliamentary acceptance of a new law in 1858, giving unmarried adult women legal majority (Burman 2001, 392). Education is another central theme in the novel. The protagonist, Hertha, funds a new school for higher education of women, and when Högre lärarinneseminariet was founded in 1861 (Ullman 2004, 34), it seemed like a realisation of the utopian women's academy in *Hertha*. In a letter from 1861, Bremer claims to have achieved her goals with *Hertha:* "My Hertha has done her work, [and?] the women of Sweden are now entit[led] to majority at the age of 25 years; and [close] to my dwelling is opened a great [semi]nary, supported by the government, [where] young women eager f[or knowledge] and truth are *freely* adm[itted] and freely tought [=taught]" (Burman 2001, 393). In connection with its opening, Fredrika Bremer made a large donation of books, and also included a statue of Iduna, the goddess of youth in Norse mythology, which also appears in Bremer's novel *Hertha* (Burman 2001, 455f). For the students at Högre lärarinneseminariet, Fredrika Bremer's heritage was a tangible one. A woman who attended the seminar in 1862 wrote to Lagerlöf in 1909. During the time, she claims to have met Fredrika Bremer. "[I]t seems to me, that nobody has shown such an understanding of this noble woman, as you do in your beautiful prose-poem," she writes (Concordia Löfving, 12 May 1909), alluding to "Mamsell Fredrika." Besides opening the path of education for women, Lagerlöf uses the example of Fredrika Bremer to show the important tasks the unmarried women can fulfil in society. Instead of telling tales for her own children—like the older female relatives Lagerlöf often evokes in her own stories—Bremer has told them to thousands, she has fought prejudice and spoken her opinion on the important questions of humanity. When writing "Mamsell Fredrika" Lagerlöf's career was just at its beginning. She had not yet told tales for thousands of children, as she did in *Christ Legends* (1904) and *The Wonderful Adventures of Nils* (1907–1908), neither had she participated in debates or political life. But her position as an author in public became closely associated with the same values that she connects to Fredrika Bremer in this story: social responsibility, an ethical obligation to help those in need and to fight for peace and equality.

The Bremer–Lagerlöf Connection in the Letters to Selma Lagerlöf

The most common connection between Fredrika Bremer and Selma Lagerlöf made in the letters to her is the Fredrika Bremer Association, which was the largest organization within the women's movement until the beginning of the suffrage movement in 1903. The principal aim of the Fredrika Bremer Society was to "promote the advancement of women morally, intellectually, socially, and economically" (Manns 2004, 153). On the initiative of Sophie Adlersparre, a fund was established in 1887, where women could apply for money, mainly for education. The Fredrika Bremer Association also administered other funds, which were established after donations from private persons. A common denominator for these was that they were directed at single, educated women, particularly teachers who could apply for money for education or recreation. Since Selma Lagerlöf's connections with important persons in the Fredrika Bremer Association were commonly known, it was not unusual that women wrote to her, asking her to help gain approval for their applications.

But the links between Bremer and Lagerlöf are more explicitly stated as well. In one letter written in January 1912, the sender explains why she turns to Selma Lagerlöf to apply for money:

Today, when I sat looking into the darkness, and couldn't see any way out, the thought occurred to me: "If Fredrika Bremer was alive, I would turn to her and she would help me." But it was just as impossible as everything else I had tried. But this thought was followed by another. It was as if somebody had whispered to me: "Selma Lagerlöf is alive." My heart beat wildly and there was a flash before my eyes, but I knew that if there was one person in the world who would understand me and want to help me, it was you. (Märta André, 29 January 1912)

Like many other letters, this one contains a life narrative, not unlike the one told by Selma Lagerlöf in "Two Prophecies." It is a story about a family in financial trouble, and the letter writer, who is the oldest daughter, is forced to work as a maid to support her younger siblings. After years of hard work, she begins at a teacher training school, with support from some friends of the family. When they too run out of money she sees no way out—"I have to get back to my former life." Her description of the captivity in this traditional female role as housemaid resembles the grim alternative imagined by the young Selma—governess in another family's home. Marriage is not an option in either of the narratives. What they instead put up against each other is enslaving spinsterhood, with no possibilities of independence, as well as the life of a single, educated woman with her own income, but also a responsibility of educating new generations of women. In this letter Fredrika Bremer and Selma Lagerlöf stand out as examples of authors taking a social responsibility for women less fortunate than themselves. The public *ethos* of both Selma Lagerlöf and Fredrika Bremer is to a large extent comprised of the same parts: being unmarried, engaged in education, and taking active part in changing women's lives.

There are also occasional critiques of Lagerlöf's utopian vision of Fredrika Bremer in "Mamsell Fredrika." In a letter from 1909 a woman tells at length of her reading of Selma Lagerlöf's work. She expresses great admiration for the stories in *Invisible Links,* and is delighted to read about Fredrika Bremer in "Mamsell Fredrika." But afterwards she re-evaluates her reading of the story. She does not approve of the idea that Fredrika Bremer has forever opened the door for all the unmarried women enslaved in the households. "I need that kind of elderly, friendly women, existing in my childhood, with outmoded hats, flowery wool dresses, and with a sense of reason and responsibility. Why did she take them away?" (Eva Linder, 28 January 1909). In this letter, the sender cannot reconcile the modern, feminist aspect of "Mamsell Fredrika" with Selma Lagerlöf's public ethos as storyteller, narrating and preserving the past. The letter writer focuses on what she perceives as a Christian way of life, represented in many of Lagerlöf's texts, which in this case is not in agreement with the promotion of women's emancipation, visible in "Mamsell Fredrika."

The freedom coming with education and professional life is underlined in many letters to Selma Lagerlöf. On her fiftieth birthday in 1908, Selma Lagerlöf's received a letter from Anna Linder and "the teachers in Landskrona." Anna Linder was a teacher at the elementary school in Landskrona, where Selma Lagerlöf had begun her professional career in 1885. The letter describes what could be called subversive feminist activities, inspired by Selma Lagerlöf. Linder begins her letter by reminding Selma Lagerlöf of the telegram she has received from the women teachers at the Landskrona seminar. "It is first and foremost a proof of our admiration for you, but also of love of freedom." She writes that the female students wanted to sign it too, but this proved to be impossible without telling the principal, Nils Torpsson. The letter is thus a complimentary greeting from the female teachers and students, written without the knowledge of the principal. Anna Linder also tells Lagerlöf about their celebrations, though they had to be "modest." "When the principal had left, we were free," she writes. "The principal cannot stand that you have become renowned, despite being a woman." In secrecy, they gather to read about Lagerlöf in different magazines, and to read a newly written text, still unprinted. It is "Two Prophecies," which Anna Linder had been allowed to copy by hand from Lagerlöf's friend in Landskrona, Anna Oom. She states that the text strongly affected the girls: "At times they had to embrace each other to give air to their emotions."

The letter describes a semi-public female culture, not unlike the romantic salon. Texts are read, discussed, and a dialogue with the author becomes possible through the letters. Anna Linder also reads a letter from Selma Lagerlöf to the students; her words about Lagerlöf's life at the seminar made a deep impression, according to Linder. Finally she asks Lagerlöf to write something for the institutions preparing women to be teachers. Linder argues that the best way to make "freedom...prevail there, even for women" is to "allow women to become principals" (Anna Linder, 22 November 1908). In the same year Anna Linder wrote two articles in *Dagny* presenting arguments supporting the proposal to allow women to be principals of the seminars educating women teachers. Briefly, her argument rests upon the assumption of specific female qualities that enable a better understanding of the needs and interests of young women, and can lead to a more democratic and less authoritative leadership (Linder 1908, 587–90, 602–603).

Women Celebrating Lagerlöf

Selma Lagerlöf's Nobel Prize was not only celebrated traditionally by the Swedish Academy, but also with a feast for women at Grand Hotel Royal in Stockholm (Stenberg 2009, 311–13; Pipping and Olsson). Lagerlöf's award was received as a victory for women at large; for those fighting for more powerful positions in public life. Märta Tamm-Götlind, leader of the Swedish section of the Women's International League for Peace and Freedom, later reported that there were not enough places for any men. "If men the wanted to attend, they had to accept employment as waiters" (Tamm-Götlind 1941, 117). Märta Tamm-Götlind, who was a student at the time, also describes Selma Lagerlöf's speech, where she thanked Fredrika Bremer. She read a part of "Mamsell Fredrika," and then went on to elaborate on how Fredrika Bremer might have perceived the celebration if she had been present. She would have found many causes to rejoice—"there were women leading large enterprises, women doctors, women leading schools and other institutions, women in a multitude of professions" (Tamm-Götlind 1941, 119). The celebration at the Royal was also reported in the press, most importantly in *Dagny* under the headline "Selma Lagerlöf and our celebration." "Women conceived it, women planned it and organized it, a woman was in charge of the magnificent assembly room, it was women who made speeches and paid tribute,—and it was a Swedish woman, known and honoured as a queen in—and outside of—our country, who was the guest of honour" (*Dagny* 1909, No. 48, 575). And with a reference to "Mamsell Fredrika" the writer continues: "Indeed, the era of the women locked within the crammed walls of the home and the overlooked and forgotten old maids are over, 'the last one' of them finally ended it" (576). Both in the report in *Dagny* and in Märta Tamm-Götlind's later memory of the occasion, the celebration is described as a quite extraordinary event, changing the history of women.

Lydia Wahlström's speech at the celebrations at the Royal, as reported in *Dagny*, also underlines Selma Lagerlöf's importance, not only as an author representing a feminist heritage, but also taking part in the creation of a new reality for women:

> And then Lydia Wahlström speaks, expressing the gratitude from the children, to whom she has given *Nils Holgersson*. From the country women, who also "know Selma." Thanks for her important contribution to in the burning question for women, the right to vote. [...] Thanks from the old women, who smile happily when she conjures up the memories from their childhood and youth. Thanks from the young women; from the suffering. (*Dagny* 1909, no. 48, 575)

Both Wahlström and Tamm-Götlind place Lagerlöf in a contemporary and social reality, which makes her works seem less like a retelling of old tales and legends, and more like a platform for social critique and social change. The reports from the celebration at the Royal also highlight the semi-public places where much of Selma Lagerlöf's professional life took place. The event at the Royal was open to anyone who bought a ticket (although women had priority over men), but it was clearly directed at a specific audience of women engaged in the question of women's rights in society. Lagerlöf's biographer, the author and feminist Elin Wägner, was herself one of the participants in the women's celebration at the Royal and recollects the event in the second part of the biography: "We were proud of Selma, and we liked her for always showing that we could count on her as one of the fighting women in Sweden" (Wägner 1943, 76).

Women Listening to Lagerlöf

Another important public event is Selma Lagerlöf's participation in the Sixth Convention of the International Women's Suffrage Alliance, in Stockholm in 1911. Her speech "Home and State" is the most influential of Lagerlöf's political statements. In short, Selma Lagerlöf argues for women's equal citizenship by pointing out the state built by men as a failure, precisely because it lacks the contribution of women. She compares men's creation of the state with women's creation of the home, and can in this way show what the state lacks—the abilities and competences coming from women's life experience (Lagerlöf 1911). Like "Mamsell Fredrika," "Home and State" points to a different evaluation of women's work, which is not connected to motherhood in its biological sense. Both Ellen Kleman, reporting on the conference in *Dagny* (1911, No. 26, 308), and Märta Tamm-Götlind's later autobiographical account of the event surrounding Lagerlöf's appearance stress the deep silence during the speech and the overwhelming acclaim afterwards. It is evident that Lagerlöf's engagement in the women's movement is more obvious to the historian than the literary scholar. Lagerlöf published few texts on the subject, but it is clearly visible in documentation such as that of Kleman and Tamm-Götlind, and in the letters to and from Selma Lagerlöf. Elin Wägner writes in her biography that the delegates from the 22 participating nations all knew Selma Lagerlöf. She was a less experienced speaker than the others—Reverend Anna Shaw, Rosika Schwimmer and Ethel Snowden—but the fact that she, as a famous author and estate owner, "lacked the rights as a citizen, which the most common male writer and farmer had thanks to his sex" made a deep impression (Wägner 1943, 85). Her mentioning of the delegates from twenty-two nations "who all knew Selma Lagerlöf" and Selma Lagerlöf's position among the other speakers is important for the social context of her works that remains to be construed, acknowledging her international reach and exchange with women in Europe and America engaged in education, the peace movement and the suffrage movement. Selma Lagerlöf seems to be a clear example of a literary celebrity "whose works and personal example served to call into existence 'virtual communities', international in scope and significance" (McFadden 1999, 4)

As I have shown elsewhere (Bergenmar 2014), Lagerlöf's standpoint in "Home and State" is connected to the writings of other European feminists. The Austrian feminist Rosa Mayreder was introduced to a Swedish audience in *Dagny* in 1910. An excerpt from the Swedish translation of Mayreder's *Zur Kritik der Weiblichkeit*, published in English as *A Survey of the Woman Problem*, is also included in the issue.[6] In the text published in *Dagny* 1910 she follows a similar line of argument as Lagerlöf in "Home and State" when she links the crisis of civilization to the lack of women's involvement in public life: "Perhaps the appearance of woman as a social fellow-worker may create a change in that field where the one-sided masculine civilization has failed" (Mayreder 1913; Schwartz 2008, 70). The Swedish translation of *Zur Kritik der Weiblichkeit* was reviewed favourably by Ellen Kleman in a later issue of *Dagny*. Kleman foregrounded Mayreder's critique of the general assumption of motherhood as woman's destiny (Kleman 1910, 294–295). Yet, it is not only the similarities between Lagerlöf's argument and other European feminists that is notable. It is the event itself, constructing a public sphere where women were included, and had the power to set the agenda. Discussing memory in contrast to canonized history, Maria Grever and Kees Ribbens remark that "[w]omen's associations, exhibitions, newspapers and institutions became a locus where women could try out new combinations of participatory and representative citizenship" (Grever and Ribbens 2008, 254). The feelings elicited by the speech and reported by Kleman, Tamm-Götlind and Wägner are also significant. In contrast to the speech itself, the emotional response to it is not a historical document, but reflected in the testimony of other participants. The two first—Kleman and Tamm-Götlind—may well be regarded as anecdotal. However, at the same time, they leave a trace of the emotions evoked by Lagerlöf's speech not easily attainable through other sources.

Teaching the Nation
While the celebration at Hotel Royal after Lagerlöf's Nobel Prize and the reports of her speech at the Convention of the International Women's Suffrage Alliance in Stockholm places Lagerlöf in a feminist context and network, there is one aspect of her role as an author not present in these events—

---

6 Notably, the Swedish translation was published two years before the English one under the title *Kvinnlighet, manlighet, mänsklighet*, authorized translation from German by Olga Andersson (1910).

Lagerlöf as teacher. "A national disaster" Ellen Key called the textbook used for elementary school (*Läsebok för folkskolan*), used in different versions since 1868. A new edition published in 1890 did not satisfy those engaged in progressive pedagogy (Ahlström 1942, 33). Key criticized the selection of literature, which in her opinion was comprised of fables and didactic stories deprived of any connection to the child's imagination, feeling and experience (Key 1898). Not only Ellen Key was dissatisfied. An initiative to produce a new schoolbook was taken by the teacher and liberal politician Fridtjuv Berg and Alfred Dahlin, an educator engaged in national school issues. They engaged authors to produce good-quality literary texts for educational use. Selma Lagerlöf was asked and accepted, but had considerable doubts about the plan—a combination of shorter stories, tales and legends, epic poems and geographical texts, some of them in literary form. Lagerlöf's own suggestion was a novel, bringing Swedish geography to life and giving readers a sense of their own people and country and its well-known outcome *The Wonderful Adventures of Nils* (1907–1908). The aesthetic aspect was important for Selma Lagerlöf—the story was to be fictive to capture the interest of the readers, but the information on different parts of Sweden had to be accurate.

The same pedagogical ambitions are present in various descriptions of her practice as a teacher. In Wägner's biography she is described as an unruly teacher: she smiled during the morning prayer, thought that the girls should be allowed to laugh during the lessons, questioned the truths of the schoolbooks, and introduced excursions and outdoor lessons (Wägner 1942, 91). In a letter to her successor as teacher in Landskrona, Ester Nennes, Lagerlöf complains about how the available textbook in religion bored her (in Carlsson 2009, 105). A former pupil testifies that her lectures were captivating. In the small schoolroom referred to as "the cave," she "opened door after door to us, and vast, new areas appeared both within us and outside of us—in the whole wide world, in the whole wide universe" (Romanus-Alfvén 1941, 49). Besides this new pedagogical approach, Romanus-Alfvén also describes how Lagerlöf taught medieval history, known by the students as a particularly tedious chapter in history. But Selma Lagerlöf focused on the queens instead of the kings, and—according to the same principle as in *The Wonderful Adventures of Nils Holgersson*—fictionalized while, at the same time, keeping the facts accurate. This new take on Swedish history could also be interpreted as an alternate telling of the nation, where women were allowed to play the leading parts. Similar experiences of being told an enchanting story rather than a factual lesson are commonly reported in the many letters to Selma Lagerlöf from teachers thanking her for *Nils Holgersson* and other texts. But another interesting aspect also appears in the letters. For the women teachers writing to her, her role as a celebrated author is, so to speak, outweighed by her role as a teacher. "It is not to the great authoress, one of the 18 in the Swedish Academy I dare to write, but to the former seminarist, the loyal friend of the schoolmistresses," a woman begins a letter pleading on behalf of a German colleague in need of financial help (Amy von Arbin, 28 June 1920). The shared experience of being a woman teacher brought this part of Lagerlöf's audience particularly close to her.

A long time had passed since Lagerlöf was a seminarist. However, to the women teachers she remained in some sense one of them. The letters also show that the social change described in "Mamsell Fredrika" was not easily carried out. Many of the women teachers writing to Selma Lagerlöf had indeed escaped the fate of becoming "mamsells." Instead they were in most cases unmarried, but educated and employed. In spite of this, the letters applying for financial aid are as common as the ones thanking Selma Lagerlöf for her contribution to schoolchildren's reading. There are two categories—young women, much in the position of the young Selma in "Two Prophecies," asking for money to afford to train to become professional teachers, and older women, not able to work as teachers due to age or health factors. In a short text published in *Dagny* 1912, Selma Lagerlöf draws the reader's attention to the conditions for women working as teachers. She does so in her usual way—through a literary style, explicitly addressing the reader as a former pupil, although the title applies a more factual rhetoric: "Home for aged schoolmistresses. A call for fundraising." Lagerlöf describes the teacher's work as unappreciated, representing dull and monotonous lessons and discipline. But then she conjures up the women teachers as individuals, not only as representatives of their profession. She tells the readers/pupil, that they couldn't possibly have known how small the salary was and how impossible it was to save money for retirement. The former pupils are induced to think about what they would have been without the hard work of their old schoolmistresses. The text ends with a plea for money to fund the building of homes for the old women teachers who can't afford households of their own. The text is signed "Your old schoolmistresses, through Selma Lagerlöf" (Lagerlöf 1912). At the time of the publication of this text, Selma Lagerlöf had won the Nobel Prize and was at the height of her career. Even so, she publicly identifies with the role of the woman teacher, and in this way contributes a public answer to all the private letters to her from women teachers in need of financial support.

The text discussing the need of homes for elderly schoolmistresses represents a dialogue between the public (of published text) and the private
(the letters). The text cannot be properly understood without the letters to
Selma Lagerlöf from the poorly paid women teachers who were unable to
save money for their pension. Her own experience as a young woman facing
financial and family obstacles for obtaining an education was echoed in the
letters to her from young women needing a loan to finance their education,
and received a public answer in "Two Prophecies."

The author as teacher also displays herself in the celebration of Lagerlöf's
fiftieth birthday 1908. It was celebrated in Falun, where Lagerlöf lived at the
time. She did not want a pompous formal ceremony; instead the celebration
was made by Sweden's schoolchildren. Elin Wägner states that many schools
all over the country took a break from the ordinary schedule after lunch that
day, and that the rest of the day was dedicated to different kinds of celebrations. In Falun, 200 pupils from the girl's school came to Lagerlöf's home and
sang for her. Later on, all the schoolchildren (boys and girls) were invited to
the old mission house, where Lagerlöf read aloud and distributed chocolate
bars with motifs from *The Wonderful Adventures of Nils* (Wägner 1943, 63–64).
Besides a true appreciation from teachers and children, this can obviously
also be interpreted as a way of marketing the new schoolbook as its second
part was published the year before. Nevertheless, it shows that the role of
teacher was important for Lagerlöf to incorporate into her identity as an
author. She was aware of the mechanisms of the literary market, and followed
her sales figures closely. However, it would be reductive to view her schoolbook as simply a way of gaining a new market. The experience of being a
teacher separated her from other contributors to Fridtjuv Berg's and Alfred
Dalin's schoolbook initiative—for example Verner von Heidenstam. The celebration can be interpreted as a semi-public answer to all the letters of appreciation she received from schoolchildren and their teachers.

Conclusion

The sources used in this article are mainly autobiographical and biographical: letters to Lagerlöf with clear traits of autobiography, letters from Selma
Lagerlöf narrating her own experiences, Lagerlöf's short stories, in some cases
explicitly autobiographical, such as "Two Prophecies," in others biographical,
as in "Mamsell Fredrika." Elin Wägner's biography represents a biographical master narrative about Selma Lagerlöf, while Märta Tamm-Götlind and
Anna-Clara Romanus-Alfvén produce smaller scraps of biographical nar-

ratives about her, while at the same time being autobiographical accounts of their encounters with the author. Even Wägner's biography has an auto-biographical side, as was shown in her description of herself as one in the audience listening to Lagerlöf at the Sixth Convention of the International Women's Suffrage Alliance.

"Mamsell Fredrika" proves a very important text to the many letter writers perceiving Lagerlöf as Bremer's successor, especially when it comes to trans-forming "spinsters" into citizens. Its first publication in *Dagny* honouring Bremer strengthens its political significance, as well as the reading of the text at the women's celebration of Selma Lagerlöf's Nobel Prize. Both in Lagerlöf's own speech at the Nobel Prize ceremony, and in the official speech to her by Claes Annerstedt, Bremer's heritage, so forcefully present in other sources and at other events, is silenced. The speech "Home and State" is well known, translated and thoroughly interpreted, but cannot be completely understood as a text. Its performance at the Convention of the International Women's Suffrage Alliance is what impresses Wägner, not its content. In this case, the historical event, as reported by Ellen Kleman in *Dagny* and in the (auto)bio-graphical accounts of Tamm-Götlind and Wägner, are more significant than the text itself for understanding the political aspects of Lagerlöf's role as an author. The debate article about the need for homes for elderly schoolmis-tresses is typical of the kind of texts Lagerlöf wrote for the press on specific appeals from people writing to her. In this case, no single letter asking Lager-löf to debate this question has been identified, but the difficulty of managing economically after a long life's labour as a schoolmistress is a recurring theme in the letters to Lagerlöf. The letter writers in these cases often appeal to their knowledge of Lagerlöf's own experience as an underpaid woman teacher.

Lagerlöf's own telling of her life, for example in "Two Prophecies," signi-fies a public acknowledgement of the problems central to Fredrika Bremer in *Hertha*: society's waste of women when denying them education and participa-tion in public life. The text's rhetorical construction relies on the difference established between the first person of the past and the first person narrating the story: the young Selma, narrowly escaping the gloomy prospect of becom-ing a spinster confined to the home and the family, in contrast to the famous author who at the height of her career tells the story of herself as a girl. Lager-löf, as a narrator of her own past, becomes a reader of her own experience (Smith and Watson 2010, 33). Here, she presents an exemplary story—the prophecy of the old women comes true, but the consequence is not failure.

Selma's not fitting into the female destiny is reinterpreted as a prerequisite for her success. As Jeremy D. Popkin puts it in his overview of autobiographies written by historians, "[r]eading autobiography reminds us of the possibilities we give up when we subscribe to the canons of our discipline" (Popkin 2005, 4). In the case of authors, the canon is usually comprised of the major literary work, not minor texts like "Two Prophecies" or "Mamsell Fredrika." The major canonical works of Lagerlöf, for example *Jerusalem* and the *Wonderful Adventures of Nils*, have been discussed as national novelistic projects (Thorup Thomsen 1997, 25; 2007), dealing with issues such as emigration and national identity after Norway's independence from Sweden in 1905. However, other aspects of the changing nation appear in the minor texts; here, women's right to vote, to work and to have decent working conditions appear as recurring themes. Feminist scholars have since long argued that "citizenship is more than a legal or national category of belonging" (Canning 2006, 17). Citizenship as legal rights is underscored in Bremer's *Hertha* and in Lagerlöf's "Home and State," but other categories of belonging than the national and legal appear in the transnational meeting at the Sixth Convention of the International Women's Suffrage Alliance: a belonging of the people excluded from legal rights and national privileges.

In the case of "Two Prophecies," the fictional traits are striking. Yet, there is also an autobiographical contract present as it is written in the first person and deals with known places, persons and events from Lagerlöf's life. However, it conveys not only facts about her early reading habits and so on, but also about the feelings connected to being admitted to the seminar and the fear of not being admitted. The same can be said about Wägner's and Tamm-Götlind's accounts of Lagerlöf's speech at Sixth Convention of the International Women's Suffrage Alliance—they focus not so much on the content as the emotional response of the audience. None of the sources would perhaps hold for the rigorous criticism of the traditional historian. However, as the gender historian Bonnie Smith has pointed out, the amateur history which texts such as Tamm-Götlind's and Ellen Kleman's report in *Dagny* could be characterized as, has been deemed as trivial by "scientific" male historians, often due to their personal and subjective style (Smith 1998, 6ff). The letters to Selma Lagerlöf are also personal—each presenting a scrap of a life story, resounding against Lagerlöf's own narratives and the narratives about her. "Private letters of ordinary people may articulate such aspects of society that do not appear in other sources, e.g. feelings or aspects of everyday life or even hidden functioning mechanisms of the society," Eve Annuk remarks (Annuk 2007, 6–7). Only by putting the different sources side by side do the invisible links between public and private sources, between literature, autobiography and fiction, appear, creating new contexts and re-evaluating established or canonical truths.

Returning to the concept of the archive, one might say that it allows for a more generous inclusion of sources the historian might deem too biased and trivial. In the archive—in its Foucauldian sense—cultural memories are stored, some of them, like the ones discussed in this article, neglected by research, others completely silenced. Indeed, some of the sources used here I was initially made aware of, not through research, but through archival work. Participating in a digital scholarly edition of Lagerlöf's texts, my task was to chart all the published texts written by Selma Lagerlöf that were *not* included in any book edition. These non-canonized texts pointed to another side of her authorship. They were conveying a counter-narrative to the established narrative of Selma Lagerlöf, showing her as an author concerned about the war, writing satirically about conservative men fearing the emancipated women, and making statements about women priests. Parallel to the production of the great novels ran the production of minor texts, often published in the press or in magazines, often connected to issues of current interest. This counter-narrative is also present in the letters from her audience.[7] In them, the cultural memories of the author and her time are accumulated. Howevever, these memories have hardly made any impression on the canonical narrative of the authorship.

---

7 The letters are discussed in the forthcoming book *Läsarnas Lagerlöf* (2014) by Jenny Bergenmar and Maria Karlsson, Uppsala University.

References

Unpublished
Letters to Selma Lagerlöf, National Library of Sweden, The Selma Lagerlöf Collection, L1:100
André, Märta, 29 January 1912
Arbin, Amy von, 28 June 1920
Linder, Anna, 22 November 1908
Linder, Eva, 28 January 1909
Löfving, Concordia, 12 May 1909

Published
Adlersparre, S. 1891. "En blick på Fredrika Bremer och hennes lifsgärning. Af Esselde." *Dagny. Tidskrift för litterära och sociala intressen*, no. 1–2: 5–27.
Ahlström, G. 1942. *Den underbara resan: En bok om Selma Lagerlöfs Nils Holgersson*. Lund: Gleerup.
Annerstedt, C. 1909. In *Nobel Lectures: Literature 1901–1969*. Edited by Horst Frenz. Amsterdam: Elsevier Publishing Company, 1969, http://www.nobelprize.org/nobel_prizes/literature/laureates/1909/press.html.
Annuk, E. 2007. "Letters as a New Approach to History: A Case Study of an Estonian Poet Ilmi Kolla (1933–1954)." *Nordic Journal of Women's Studies*, no. 1: 6–20.
Bagerius, H. 2011. "Historikern och skönlitteraturen," *Moderna historier: Skönlitteratur i det moderna samhällets framväxt*, edited by Henric Bagerius and Ulrika Lagerlöf Nilsson, 17–32. Lund: Nordic Academic Press.
Bergenmar, J. 2003. *Förvildade hjärtan: Kärlekens estetik och berättandets etik i Selma Lagerlöfs Gösta Berlings saga*. Dissertation Göteborg. Stockholm/Stehag: Symposion.
———. 2014 "Selma Lagerlöf, Fredrika Bremer and Women as Nation Builders." In *Telling the Nation*, edited by A. Sanz, S. van Dijk, and F. Scott. Amsterdam: Rodopi Editions.
Bohlin, A. 2008. *Röstens anatomi: Läsningar av politik i Elin Wägners Silverforsen, Selma Lagerlöfs Löwensköldstrilogi och Klara Johanssons Tidevarvskåserier*. Dissertation, Umeå: h:ström.
Burman, C. 2001. *Bremer: En biografi*. Stockholm: Bonniers.
Canning, K. 2006. *Gender History in Practice: Historical Perspectives on Bodies, Class and Citizenship*. Ithaca: Cornell University Press.
Carlsson, L, ed. 2009. *Selma, Anna och Elise: Brevväxling mellan Selma Lagerlöf,*

92 JENNY BERGENMAR

Anna Oom och Elise Malmros åren 1886–1913. Del 1. 1886–1913. Landskrona: Litorina.

———. ed. 2010. *Selma, Anna och Elise: Brevväxling mellan Selma Lagerlöf, Anna Oom och Elise Malmros åren 1914–1937. Del 2. 1914–1937.* Landskrona: Litorina.

Claesson Pipping, G., and T. Olsson. 2010. *Dyrkan och spektakel: Selma Lagerlöfs framträdanden i offentligheten i Sverige 1909 och Finland 1912.* Stockholm: Carlssons.

Cvetkovic, A. 2009. *An Archive of Feelings: Trauma, Sexualities, and Lesbian Public Cultures.* Durham and London: Duke University Press.

Danbolt, M., J. Rowley, and L. Wolthers. 2009. *Lost and Found: Queerying the Archive.* Copenhagen: Nikolaj Copenhagen Contemporary Art Centre.

Darnton, R. 1986. "First Steps towards a History of Reading." *Australian Journal of French Studies* 23(1): 5–30.

Edström, V. 2002. *Selma Lagerlöf: Livets vågspel.* Stockholm: Natur och kultur.

Englund, B. and Kåreland, L. 2008. *Rätten till ordet: En kollektivbiografi över skrivande Stockholms-kvinnor 1880–1920.* Stockholm: Carlssons.

Foucault, M. 1972. *The Archaeology of Knowledge and the Discourse on Language.* Translated by A. M. Sheridan Smith. New York: Pantheon Books.

Grever, M., and K. Ribbens. 2008. "The Dynamics of Memories and the Process of Canonization." In *The Gender of Memory: Cultures of Remembrance in Nineteenth- and Twentieth-Century Europe*, 253–265. Frankfurt and New York: Campus.

Halldórsdóttir, E. A. "Fragments of Lives—The Use of Private Letters in Historical Research." *Nora. Nordic Journal of Feminist and Gender Research* no. 1: 35–49.

Iddeng, J. W. 2005. "Litteratur som historisk kilde." *Historisk tidsskrift* 84(3).

Karlsson, M. 2002. *Känslans röst: Det melodramatiska i Selma Lagerlöfs romankonst.* Dissertation, Uppsala. Stockholm/Stehag: Symposion.

Key, E. 1898. "Patriotismen och läseböckerna." *Ord och Bild*, no. 7: 136–144.

Kleman, E. 1910. "Kvinnlighet, manlighet, mänsklighet: Essayer af Rosa Mayreder. Rec. Af E. K-n." *Dagny*, no. 25: 294–295.

———. 1911. "Den internationella rösträttskonferensen." *Dagny*, no. 25: 294–295.

Lagerlöf, S. 1891. "Mamsell Fredrika." *Dagny*, no. 1–2: 28–35. Also in *Invisible Links* [1894], translated by Pauline Bancroft Flach, Boston: Little Brown & Company, 1899. Available online at www.openlibrary.org/books/OL14015398M/Invisible_links.

————. 1908. "Två spådomar [Two Prophecies]: Ett stycke lefvnadsteckning."
Bonniers månadshäften 2: 795–810.

————. 1911. *Home and State*. Translated by Velma Swanston Howard.

————. 1912. *"Åldersdomshem för svenska lärarinnor.* Ett upprop om penningeinsamling [Home for Elderly Schoolmistresses. A Call for Fundraising]."
Dagny, no. 20: 234.

————. 1924 [1922]. *Mårbacka*. Translated by Velma Swanston Howard. New
York: Doubleday, Page & Company.

————. 1934 [1930]. *Memories of my Childhood: Further Years at Marbacka*. Translated by Velma Swanston Howard. New York: Doubleday, Doran.

————. 1936 [1932]. *The Diary of Selma Lagerlöf.* Translated by Velma Swanston
Howard. New York: Doubleday, Doran.

Linder, A. 1908. "Reformtankar i skolfrågor." *Dagny*, no. 46–47: 587–590,
602–603.

Manns, U. 2004. "Gender and Feminism in Sweden: The Fredrika Bremer
Association." In *Women's Emancipation Movements in the 19th Century: A European Perspective*, 152–164. Stanford: Stanford University Press.

McFadden, M. H. 1999. *The Golden Cables of Sympathy: The Transatlantic Sources
of Nineteenth-Century Feminism*. Lexington: University Press of Kentucky.

Nordlund, A. 2005. *Selma Lagerlöfs underbara resa genom den svenska litteraturhis-
torien 1891–996*. Dissertation, Uppsala. Stockholm: Symposion.

Pascoe, A. H. 2004. "Literature as Historical Archive." *New Literary History* 3:
373–394.

Petersens, L. af. 2006. *Formering för offentlighet: Kvinnokonferenser och Svenska
kvinnornas nationalförbund kring sekelskiftet 1900*. Dissertation, Stockholm.
Stockholm: Stockholm Studies in History.

Popkin, J. D. 2005. *History, Historians and Autobiography*. Chicago and London:
Chicago University Press.

Romanus-Alfvén, A.-C. 1941. "Några lektioner för Selma Lagerlöf." In *Mårbacka och Övralid: Minnen av Selma Lagerlöf och Verner von Heidenstam*, 49–66.
Första samlingen. Uppsala: J.A. Lindblads förlag.

Schwarts, A. 2008. *Shifting Voices: Feminist Thought and Women's Writing in Fin-
de-siècle*. Quebec: McGill-Queen University Press.

————. 1909. "Selma Lagerlöf och vår fest." *Dagny*, no. 48: 575–576.

Smith, S., and J. Watson. 2010. *Reading Autobiography: A Guide for Interpreting
Life Narratives*. 2nd edition. Minneapolis: University of Minnesota Press.

Stanley, L. 2004. "The Epistolarium: On Theorizing Letters and Correspond-
ences." *Auto/Biography* no. 12: 201–235.

Stenberg, L. 2002. *En genialisk lek: Kritik och överskridanden i Selma Lagerlöfs tidiga författarskap.* Dissertation, Göteborg. Göteborg: Skrifter utgivna av Litteraturvetenskapliga institutionen vid Göteborgs universitet.

————. 2009. *I kärlekens namn: Människosynen, den nya kvinnan och framtidens samhälle i fem litteraturdebatter 1881–1909.* Stockholm: Normal.

Smith, B. 1998. *The Gender of History: Men, Women and Historical Practice.* Cambridge, MA: Harvard University Press.

Tamm-Götlind, M. 1941. "Selma Lagerlöfs framtidsprogram. Några festliga minnen från 'stora' dagar." In *Mårbacka och Övralid: Minnen av Selma Lagerlöf och Verner von Heidenstam.* Ny samling, edited by Sven Thulin. Uppsala: J.A. Lindblads förlag.

Thomsen, B. T. 1997. "Aspects of Topography in Selma Lagerlöf's *Jerusalem,* vol. 1." *Scandinavica* 36: 23–41.

————. 2007. *Lagerlöfs litterære landvinding: Nation, mobilitet og modernitet i Nils Holgersson og tilgrænsende tekster.* Amsterdam: Scandinavisch Instituut, Universiteit van Amsterdam.

Toijer-Nilsson, Y, ed. 2006. *En riktig författarhustru: Selma Lagerlöf skriver till Valborg Olander.*

Ullman, A. 2004 *Stiftarinnegenerationen: Sofi Almquist, Anna Sandström, Anna Ahlström.* Stockholm: Stockholmia förlag.

Wägner, Elin. 1942. *Selma Lagerlöf 1. Från Mårbacka till Jerusalem.* Stockholm: Bonnier.

————. *Selma Lagerlöf 2. Från Jerusalem till Mårbacka.* Stockholm: Bonnier.

Wijkmark, S. 2009. *Hemsökelser: Gotiken i sex berättelser av Selma Lagerlöf.* Dissertation, Karlstad. Karlstad: Karlstad University Studies 20.

Emancipation and the New Woman in Early Estonian Journalism

*Eve Annuk**

Abstract

The article analyzes the ideas of gender in late nineteenth century Estonian public discourse—mostly in Estonian newspapers, but also in the first Estonian feminist magazine *Linda* as well as certain literary texts. The question of women's emancipation became relevant in Estonia in the second half of the nineteenth century. The discussion in Estonian-language newspapers focused primarily on women's education, but it highlighted different attitudes towards women's role and position in society and in the domestic sphere as well. The discussion can be characterized as relying on a belief in the different natural roles of women and men that are reflected in contemporary social arrangements: women were seen in the context of the private sphere, men in the context of the public sphere. As a result, it was thought that women's education was to prepare her for taking care of the household and children, while giving only limited skills that would enable them to work outside the home. This attitude was also shared by the leaders of Estonian national movement, such as Carl Robert Jakobson and Jakob Hurt.

Despite more radical gender ideas expressed by first Estonian feminist Lilli Suburg, the overall discussion stayed within the limits of the conservative concept of gender of the period. However, the question of women's emancipation found a more responsive audience at the beginning of the twentieth century, in the context of the revolutionary movements of 1905 when, in addition to women's education, attention shifted to women's civil rights.

Introduction

The article deals with ideas about gender and women's emancipation in Estonian public discourse—primarily in newspapers but also in the first Estonian feminist magazine *Linda* as well as in certain literary texts at the end of the

* Dr. Eve Annuk is a senior researcher of Estonian literature at the Estonian Cultural History Archives in the Estonian Literary Museum. The article was written with the support of the targeted research projects *Sources of Cultural History and the Contextuality of Literature* (SF0030065s08) and *Formal and Informal Networks of Literature, Based on Sources of Cultural History* (IUT22-2) and Estonian Science Foundation grant no. 8875 *Gender Question in Estonia: Local Situation and International Influences.*

nineteenth century. The printed media had a considerable influence on shaping the attitudes of the readers and thereby also shaping public consciousness.
Radical ideas spread through the press and Estonian readers were informed
about both the women's movement that had gained a considerable position in
other European countries, as well as ideas concerning female emancipation.

The article discusses the relation between the Estonian national movement and women's emancipation, since the national movement considerably
shaped the gender attitudes which were adopted by the intelligentsia and
used in Estonian national ideology remaining virtually unchanged throughout the twentieth century.

The article will start with a survey of the Estonian newspapers and the
issues they dealt with, concerning gender. Such a survey is new up until now
and therefore it is an important part of the aim of the article. Themes of
women's education and emancipation are explored. Thereafter the feminist
Lilli Suburg and her magazine Linda is analysed, as well as Suburg's concept
of gender concerning the idea of a new woman. The analysis attempts to find
the answers to questions such as what ideas and actors dominated the gender
discourse at the end of nineteenth century in Estonia. Also, how was gender
connected to nationalism and what was the role of the new Estonian woman
to be?

**Ideology concerning Gender in the Baltics and in Estonia at the End of
the Nineteenth Century**
The Baltic countries retained a conservative concept of gender for a long
period of time due to both a lack of development in comparison with the
Western or Northern European countries and the cultural influence of the
Baltic Germans.[1] The ideology concerning gender that was established in the
mid-nineteenth century in the Baltic countries stressed gender differences
and determined the domain of women to be the domestic sphere. Although
men were assigned a role in the public sphere, economy and politics, while
women were assigned a role in family and at home, these different gender
roles were seen as dependent on, and complimenting, each other. This ideology concerning gender came from the German bourgeoisie and spread to

---

1 Discussions on gender reached the Baltic countries through Europe as the women's movement
became prominent in Europe at the end of the nineteenth century and a broad spectrum of feminist
ideologies and activities, such as international women's congresses, sufragettes movement etc.
developed (Fuchs and Thompson 2005, 167–168). Thus, feminism was a part of intellectual culture in
Europe at the end of nineteenth century (ibid, 176).

the Baltic provinces where German cultural influence was strong (Whelan 1999, 111).

A conservative concept of gender was one of the cornerstones of the world-view of the Baltic German nobility; as such, it was embedded into all strata of society (Whelan 1995, 173). For the Baltic Germans, the role of a woman was connected to a family cult shared by people of different social status: *literati*, nobility as well as burgesses (Whelan 1999, 113). The family was the embodi-ment of the German nation and its spirit, and it was regarded as something holy. The wife—*Hausfrau*—was the centre of family life and the private sphere, since, as opposed to the masculine rationality and association with public sphere, she represented emotionality (Whelan 1995, 165, 167). A culture of "true home-centred femininity," motherhood being one aspect of it, devel-oped hand-in-hand with the family cult. In addition to the feminine qualities, women needed to possess a number of virtues such as patience, obedience, submissiveness, modesty, virtuousness, purity, selflessness etc. (Whelan 1999, 117; 1995, 167). Furthermore, women were required to assist their husbands, which required that they acquired a number of Christian virtues. Child-like faith in God and religious dedication were part of being a woman. Lack of the fear of God in women was regarded as a deficiency (Whelan 1995, 168). The cult of femininity and the ideology concerning gender dominated through-out the nineteenth century and every attempt to challenge it was assiduously countered by the conservative priests, teachers and nobility, who in every gen-der related claim saw an attack on the divine order (Whelan 1995, 168; 1999, 234).

The social historian Heide Whelan claims that the demands concerning gender equality started spreading in the Baltic countries following the exam-ple of the women's rights movements of the 1860s in England, Russia and Germany. Although the women's movement had little influence in the Baltic provinces, its call to change the social power structures was still regarded as dangerous (Whelan 1995, 169). The Baltic women's movement was more similar to the German women's movement than to those in Russia, Great Brit-ain or America because, similarly to the German women's movement, it lim-ited its goals to a demand to integrate women into the work force, whereas the goals of the women's movements in other countries had a strong politi-cal dimension. Similarly to Germany, the women's movement of the Baltic Germans was silent in both the social as well as political sense. Since the development possibilities of women were hindered by their low educational level, gender equality demands were first and foremost connected to women's education, because the "requirements of an expanding capitalism" expected women to work outside their homes as well (Whelan 1995, 180).

The Issue of Women's Emancipation and The National Movement
The concept of gender of the Baltic Germans influenced the views of the lower classes, who adopted and adjusted it to their own needs. Even the intellectual elites of nineteenth century Estonia, both those who were germanised and the supporters of Estonian national identity, adopted "the dominating bourgeois moral code that in addition to the segregation mechanisms existing in village culture, lay foundations to the patriarchal nature of the national awakening movement" (Kivimaa 2009, 48). The Estonian national movement adopted the conservative attitude towards women's rights without questioning it (Kivimaa 2009, 41, 48). According to the historian Sirje Kivimäe, the Estonian national movement was "entirely a male enterprise;" all the large national associations were founded on the basis of male membership only, and the song festivals, central events in raising Estonian national consciousness, were closed for women until 1879 (Kivimäe 1995, 121–22). The role of women in the movement of national awakening was rather supportive, for example, women helped to organize exhibition-sales and raise funds. The absence of women in the national movement has been explained by the fact that the "patriarchy was ingrained in the Estonian society and that did not look well upon women participating in the public life" (Laar 2006, 294). The number of women taking part in the national movement grew as the movement progressed; this is why the parallel between the development of women's emancipation and national awakening went unnoticed. (Laar 2006, 295). The Estonian historian Sirje Tamul characterization of the Estonian society of the second half of the nineteenth century is not surprising: "Estonian society, which tried to follow the pattern of the German society, was even more backward regarding women's ambitions than the rest of the Europe of the Victorian era; the at times ultra-conservative mind-set lowered women into a position equal with that of a child" (Tamul 1999, 13). Despite such conservative framework, the topic of women's education became important for the people taking part in the national movement, since educated men needed educated women by their side as wives and supporters. Women as part of the national project needed to be educated in order for them to understand the goals of national movement and rear children according to the national spirit, while local German elite propagated the idea that women need education first and foremost to fulfil their role as wives and mothers (see Whelan 1995).

Keeping in mind national and agricultural interests, Estonian national leaders Carl Robert Jakobson (1841–1882) and Jakob Hurt (1839–1907) stressed
the need to raise the educational level of Estonian women even though they
were of the opinion that the right place for a woman was the home and the
family. Although they wished to further women's education they did not consider secondary education to be necessary for women (Sirk 2011, 102, 106).

Carl Robert Jakobson's ideas about the social roles of women were *petit
bourgeois* and patriarchal: he considered the task of women to be supporting
their husbands and raising children in accordance with the national spirit
(Kivimäe 1995, 124–25). Jakobson's views about women and their education
were voiced also in his newspaper articles: "In order to educate women we
need to consider their nature first. The nature of a female determines that it
is only amongst her family and in her house with her children that she finds
activities and it is only there she can experience true happiness. Therefore,
the goal in educating women must be to make a woman so skilful regarding
the family and the house, that her husband, as well as other people, will consider this family's house the most beautiful house and this family's life the
happiest possible life" (Jakobson 1881, 1). For Jakobson it was the husband
who had to work, create wealth, be active in studying new ideas and all that
in accordance with the national spirit; a woman, on the other hand, had to
take care of the home and family; a woman was pictured like a sun who does
not work herself but whose warmth gives birth to new life. Therefore the goal
of women's education was to develop a woman's family-centered nature. The
women who did not have a family of their own could contribute to the family
life, for example, by working as maids. In a reader meant for girls titled *Beads*
(1880), Jakobson followed similar conservative beliefs about the different
roles attributed to different genders that determined educational possibilities, the needs of women and limited a women's sphere of activity to the home
(see Mattheus 2008, 101–103).

An important question is thus to what extent the dominant concept of gender reach peasants whose beliefs and understandings were partly shaped by
centuries old manners and traditions yet also were affected by the new laws
that gave women an unequal position in relation to men. Aleksander Veiderma, for instance, has written in his memoires about peasants whose daughters were entitled to a much lesser part of the immovable property than sons,
and when determining the amount of bequest, dowries attributed to daughters upon their marriage were also counted as part of it (Veiderma 2000, 21).
Sirje Kivimäe has claimed that in Estonian peasant society, women were not

so much in a subordinate position as that the patriarchal attitude spread concomitantly with new ownership relations and that modernizing Estonian society followed the example of the so-called "little Germans" who deployed petit *bourgeois* attitudes, rather than those of the German high society (Kivimäe 1995, 125).

The Woman Question in Estonian Newspapers

The woman question was first covered in the Baltic German newspapers already in the mid-nineteenth century when a debate over women's education rose in a magazine published in Riga titled *Baltische Monatsschrift*: did girls need schooling in order to become ladies or housewives? The discussion continued, becoming more heated and the questions more pointed, towards the end of the century when the need for workplaces for women emerged; that in turn meant that women's education needed improvement (Lukas 2004, 151).

Estonian newspapers could not disregard the issue either. The daily *Pärnu Postimees* wrote about women's education already in 1863, stressing that mothers as the rearers of children needed to be educated. It was also pointed out that although men were poorly educated, women were even worse off: "There is almost no such thing as women's education!" Life in Estonia will not get better until women are educated in religion, hygiene, modesty, handicraft, household matters and good ways and manners (Eesti emmad 1863, 179–81).

Estonian newspapers covered the women question and women's education more frequently from 1880s onward. During this period the number of readers, as well as issues increased (Undla-Põldmäe 1981, 277). The women question was treated both by more influential newspapers such as *Eesti Postimees, Sakala, Olevik, Virulane* and *Postimees*, as well as newspapers with lesser circulation. The more innovative and democratic world-view was presented in the daily *Sakala* that was published from 1878. Short remarks as well as longer argumentative articles appeared.

These articles discussed the woman's role in the society and home, the reasons of women's poor education, possibilities for giving them a better education and the employment opportunities for women beyond their homes. The issue of women's rights was touched upon and there were articles about the situation of women in different countries as well as women's liberation movement. One of the central topics concerning the women issue was the education of women—that since the low level of education of Estonian women was becoming an obstacle for the development of the whole society. For instance, the daily *Sakala* of February 24, 1879 stressed on its front page that besides

advancing the education of men there is a more pressing need to increase the
level of women's education (P. P. 1879). The lacking circumstances of women
were attributed to their poor educational level that in turn was caused by the
overall poverty as well as the outdated attitudes (Simberg 1887; Naisterahvas
1887b).

In one of the 1880 *Sakala* articles titled "A Woman" ("Naisterahvas"), the
need to raise and educate women as mothers was stressed (-W. 1880). The
position of women throughout history and in different parts of the world,
such as the Orient and ancient Rome as opposed to the Scandinavian countries where women had more rights, was discussed in an article extending
through four issues. The article associated the loss of women's rights with the
spread of Christianity. It is because of Christianity that "the female had been
submitted to daunting, was ripped of her human dignity and value together
with the human rights and that she was forced too low both in her mind and
in overall existence" (-W 1880, no. 20, p. 1). After all, women are the "mothers of humans" and having left them without rights brought great harm both
to women themselves, as well as men and the whole humankind. The article
emphasised that the general educational level of people was dependent on
mothers and it is therefore important to educate women as mothers.

The daily *Eesti Postimees* discussed the woman issue in an article titled "The
Question of our Woman" ("Meie naisterahva küsimus"), published in 1887 as
a series in several issues of the newspaper. The article brought out the reasons
for inequality and concluded that the "wit of mind" of females was surpassed
by that of males because of upbringing (education) and not because of their
lesser natural abilities. An overview of the situation of women in different
countries was also provided. The article stresses the right of women to get
equal pay for equal work since women do not have fewer expenses than men:
"if she was to get paid more, she would obviously spend more too". To blame in
the inconsolable fate of women was an education that did not allow them to
make better choices: "But the matter lays in the fact that most women are not
thinking creatures in the ordinary sense, for they lack the necessary education for that, and, as long as things are this way, as long as we consider a complete education to be for men only, women will remain under the serfdom of
men, submitted under the rule and thumb of men and the life of a woman
will be similar to that of the life of an oriental woman" (Simberg 1887, March
21, 3). The author of the article concludes that it is only through solid education that a woman can raise the quality of her life.

The daily *Virulane* contributed to the discussion when it published a longer serial titled "A Woman" ("Naisterahvas") that contemplated over the matter of women's education. The argument is that in Estonia, as well as in the rest of Europe, it is customary to consider women inferior to men; this is why it is considered natural that women are less educated and have fewer rights. Yet the responsibilities of women as mothers and child-rearers are far bigger than the responsibilities of men, and therefore women should have greater rights and a good education to cope with her tasks. Reasons as to why the society contributes less to the education of women are brought up: it is partly due to the poverty of the society, partly due to the old-fashioned beliefs according to which education does not prepare them for life. This concerns women of both lower and higher social status. Women should be taught professions with the help of which they would manage to provide for themselves. The country-side did not, however, offer many possibilities for women to make ends meet if she is not a servant or a married woman because there were no suitable professions for women there. Therefore, many women headed for towns to find employment. However, due to the lack of suitable jobs, they often ended up in disgrace. The comparison was made between the Estonian women and women in other European countries and North America who hold various professions. The article concludes with a hope for the improvement of the situation (Naisterahvas 1887b).

Newspapers also turned their attention to the portion of female authors in the production of literature. The topic of Estonian female authors was treated in the *Virulane* in 1887 with the conclusion that the scarcity of women authors was a real shortcoming for Estonian literature (Naesterahwa töödest Eesti kirjanduses 1887a, 2). The legal situation of women was also a subject under observation, for example, the improvement of the conditions of farm-wives due to the implementation of new court system found coverage (Sõnumid isamaalt 1889, 2).

The turn of the century brought to the Estonian newspapers more frequent discussions of women's questions; the women's movement was introduced more extensively. In 1894 *Eesti Postimees* published an article "Some Words about the Contemporary Women's Movement" ("Mõnda meie aja naesterahva liikumisest"). There the international women's movement was described as a war against men. The American suffrage movement and the feats of the women in the realization of their rights were extensively covered and the nineteenth century was titled the century of freedom and victories (Mõnda meie aja naesterahva liikumisest 1894).

Estonian media covered the situation of women in different countries (Fin-

land, Sweden, Norway) comparing it to the situation in Estonia. The situation
of Estonian women was found to be considerably worse than the situation of
women in the Nordic countries. The Nordic countries were presented as positive examples of countries where women have had strong positions throughout centuries: "There is no nation in the world in which women have had
such a great amount of rights nor been honoured to such an extent than in
the Scandinavian countries during the ancient times and partly also today."
(Naesterahvas Rootsi ja Norramaal 1881, 1) The neighbouring country, Finland, was the closest example of a better situation of women. Estonian readers
were also introduced to Finnish female authors and feminists such as Minna
Canth, translator Elisabeth Löfgren, and feminist Lucina Hagman. *Olevik*
(1896) published a critical piece on the situation of Estonian women referring
to an article in a Finnish women's magazine *Koti ja Yhteiskunta* by Lilli Lilius.
Here, she had described the difficult situation of Estonian women and was
critical about the dominant ideology concerning gender in Estonia. According to Lilius, beliefs in Estonia about women were outdated and educational
possibilities limited (Eesti naisterahvas 1896).

A more conservative approach to women's issues was taken by the daily *Postimees*, which in 1892 published an article "On the Women Question" ("Naesterahva küsimusest"), treating the women's movement and voting rights in
Britain as well as women's rights in general. The article defended traditional
gender roles and claimed that the main profession for women should be marriage (-ts., 1892). In 1895 the *Postimees* published an article titled "Women
in History" ("Naesterahvas ajaloos"). Here, much in the spirit of national-
conservatism, the main area of activity for women was found to be home and
family (Naesterahvas ajaloos 1895).

Although the discussions related to women in the Estonian newspapers
brought forth different positions about the place and role of women in society and in domestic life, these usually reflected the general ideas of gender of
the period and were based on the beliefs that the different roles of men and
women were predetermined by nature. Although the necessity of educating
women in such a way would enable them to work outside the home was recognized, no fundamental changes regarding gender relations were expected.

The Topic of Emancipation in the Magazine *Linda*
More radical opinions concerning women's rights and gender roles were
brought into the discussion by the first Estonian feminist, journalist, pedagogue, and writer, Lilli Suburg (1841–1923), when she started countering

the ideology concerning gender which shaped the understanding of gender in the Baltic-German society, and which influenced the bourgeois (middle-class, literati) and *petit-bourgeois'* treatment of women and men. *Linda*, which Suburg edited from 1887–1893, gave her the opportunity to express and disseminate her ideas; true, the readership was quite limited since *Linda*'s print run during the first years was approximately 500–800 copies and there were around 300 subscribers (Annus, Loogväli 2002, 362). Since, at first, the ideology and content of the magazine were the responsibility of Suburg alone, the first three issues could be grouped under personal journalism, but the role of Suburg was also significant in the following issues (Undla-Põldmäe 1981, 281). This gave her the possibility to develop an ideological backbone for the magazine that was in accordance with her own beliefs. During the time when Suburg was the editor, the topic of emancipation was more extensively covered in *Linda* than during the later period when the magazine was edited by Heinrich Prants (officially from 1895), Anton Jürgenstein (from 1898) and Jaan Tõnisson (from 1902). Suburg's democratic ideas carried the spirit of enlightenment and shaped the content of *Linda*, giving it a specific face as a forum for female emancipation. The way Suburg dealt with gender topic often aroused negative reactions.

According to the title page specification, *Linda* was "the first literary and up-to-date magazine for Estonian women." The magazine published literary texts (poems, stories), biographies of well-known people, criticism and different opinion articles (e.g. in the editorial or main article) as well as advice on behaviour, childrearing and other issues with columns titled "School and home" ("Kodu ja Kool"), "Quarrel corner for Maidens" ("Nääklemise nurk Neidudele"), "Complaining Corner for Women" ("Nuramise nurk Naistele"), etc. Among contributors were writers Andres Rennit, Juhan Kunder, Ado Reinvald, Elise Aun and of course Lilli Suburg herself, who published a story titled "Leeni" in the magazine as well as various autobiographical prose works. *Linda* stood out by its ideological emphasis, the objective of the magazine was general-cultural: to educate and teach women and develop their thinking (Undla-Põldmäe 1981, 284).

The most important section in the magazine in its first years came to be the editorial or main article that treated the woman question (Undla-Põldmäe 1981, 284). In the editorial of the first issue of *Linda*, "A word to fellow women" ("Sõnakene suguõdedele"), Suburg called the possibility to discuss the problems of women openly in a women's magazine a "glimmer of the dawn of free-

dom." Suburg spurred women to come out "from behind the stoves," encour-
aging them to start contributing to *Linda*, despite of the fact that writing was
considered a male profession. She reassured women not to care about such
gender stereotypes according to which a woman who writes publicly would
lose her femininity and acquire a male-like nature:

> There are men even amongst our writers who think that woman's nature
> is a book with seven seals, and who immediately on the occasion of one
> of our kind uttering a sensible written word in public, will cry out loud:
> this is a manly woman; she has no gentleness and no feelings of the heart
> any longer! And so on. But these men would not even recall that these
> are the wives of our farmers who similarly to men still toil the hardest on
> the fields, meadows, barns and stables, but who nevertheless have not lost
> their gentleness (Suburg 1887a, 2).

In spurring women to aspire for education and greater freedom, Suburg concludes her call for action with an energetic "Ahead!" In the same first issue
Suburg started publishing her serial titled "Leeni, the Eternal Underling"
(Suburg 1887c), where the central themes were the problems surrounding
women's education and woman's rights—the same topics Suburg frequently
covered in other articles in *Linda*. In a way, Leeni is an ideal woman through
whom the readers are offered an example, a female role model, who possesses
a combination of wit, a patient mind, and female compassion.

Most outstanding by its tone and logic of argumentation is an editorial
titled "Emancipirt!" in *Linda* no. 7, 1888, where Suburg clarified the meaning of the term *emancipation* and called on women to educate themselves
using Western women as role models. They had, in comparison with Estonian
women, reached further in standing up for their rights. Suburg brought arguments in defence of the equal intellectual abilities of men and women, thus
contesting the existing bias against women.

Suburg contested biological determinism, which was the cornerstone of
conservative ideology concerning gender and stressed that emancipation was
"the duty of women." Suburg's understanding of emancipation was, among
other things, based on the fact that women and men are equal by their nature,
that they are inseparably connected with each other and are complimenting
each other in their differences. The point is more direct in her articles about
marriage and singleness:

If one is lacking in a necessary quality the other will have more of it; for instance, more muscle power in men and more of the tender feelings of the heart in women etc. Such a distribution of qualities bears witness to that they are meant to live side by side, not separating under any circumstance. If the latter still happens, it goes against nature and creates faulty forms of being, deficient of happiness. (Suburg 1887b, 67)

Although such a viewpoint partly reflects the conservative ideas of gender of the Baltic-Germans that similarly emphasised the interdependence of the gender roles of men and women completing each other (see Whelan 1999, 111), Suburg was more radical in her views, overcoming the differences between men and women and seeing in them a basis for gender equality. Suburg's ideal was the relationship between man and woman that was based on equal partnership. In "Emancipirt!" Suburg treats the topic of differences between men and women from a historical perspective, attributing the lesser intellectual achievements of women not to the biological differences (such as the lesser weight of the female brain), but rather to the socio-historical conditions that have hindered women's development, limiting the educational possibilities, and thus inhibiting women from putting their abilities to use. According to Suburg, women are intellectually as able as men and she protests against the determining of woman's "nature" through male needs as the assistant of men, a practice that assigns the woman's sphere of activity to be home (Suburg 1888a, 249).

Suburg treated the topic of emancipation in broad terms covering, in addition to gender issues, the topic of overcoming class differences and national emancipation. She was fighting against many a bias and injustice common to the era. For example, she tried to disentangle the outdated opinions about spinsters, stressing the importance of single women as helping hands in a family and in raising children, and she analysed social reasons behind unmarried women. Suburg published an article titled "Married Folk and Singles" ("Paarrahvas ja üksikud") in the second and third issue of *Linda*, where she treated the topic of single (aging) women. She brought out negative connotations of the word *spinster* as well as negative attitudes towards spinsters that were reflected in the society (Suburg 1887b, 67). She also stressed that married couples would hardly manage their household as well as raising and educating children without the help of single unmarried women; that was since mothers cannot substitute unmarried women as teachers in educating their children. There are several reasons why women are left single, ranging

from societal issues to personal choices; however, the most important reason for Suburg was financial stratification that made men search for wealthy
women. Furthermore, laws play a part in the phenomenon, since young men
are obliged to serve in the army, and thus a situation is created where there
are more women than men in the social demographic. Since the derogation
of single women benefits nobody, Suburg believes that this "spawn of the spirit
of brutality and darkness of the bygone times" should be discarded today as
useless (Suburg 1887b, 97–100). Marriage was among the topics that Suburg
treated. She was of the opinion that one should not marry for money or without love. A marriage should be the union of equal partners where spouses
support each other. A marriage without love is degrading for women (Suburg
1889b). What is important in a marriage is harmony concerning both mind
and spirit: "A man should not think that it is degrading for him to support
his wife in household chores and tasks, if she uses his help when none other
is available" (Suburg 1891, 196). However, one should not get married at any
cost; unmarried women can also be happy (Suburg 1890, 157).

Suburg treated moral issues in her writings and protested against double
standards. She was of the opinion that it is not right to condemn "fallen"
women since it is the men who have taken advantage of them and should be
blamed (Suburg 1888d). She also wrote about the term *beauty* from the perspective of morals and found that we should talk not only about female beauty,
but also about male beauty. It is not only the freshness of youth that makes a
woman beautiful but also experiences, love and caretaking, and hard labour
that wrinkles the face but which, precisely because of those wrinkles, deserves
to be honoured. Men become beautiful by leading a chaste lifestyle and avoiding alcohol (L. T. 1889, 166). Suburg also turned her attention to the legal status of peasant women. She pointed out that until 1889 a peasant woman could
not independently defend her rights in the court of law. She was under the
guardianship of her husband and an unmarried woman had to have a male
representative in court. The new court act gave women the right to defend
themselves in court without male guardianship (Suburg 1889a, 224–26).

There were discussions in *Linda* concerning the role of men and father-
hood. Suburg presented her view of a father as the head of a family engaged
with the children, and not the tyrant in whose presence the whole family
would fall fearfully silent. In one literary text she described to the readers
the different father figures that left no doubt as to which of them was to be
preferred. ('Three images" ["Kolm pilti"], *Linda* 1889).

Suburg connected gender emancipation to national liberation and the right to be Estonian without the feeling of inferiority. Already her first piece of writing, a short story titled "Liina," was constructed around this principle. It was exceptional for its ideological courage during a time when the general attitude was seeking reconciliation with the landlords. Suburg used *Linda* to explore the national subject more extensively (e.g. "The Critic" ["Kriitik"] 1888).

Lilli Suburg's "New Woman"
Suburg's world view united the child-raising principles of Pestalozzi and Rousseau, the world improving aspirations and love of humans of the enlightenment era, the categorical imperative of German idealist philosophy, Schiller's ideal woman, positivist environment theories, socialist criticism of society. All those even controversial elements were united by Suburg's "great love for the humankind and a sense of decency," as the literary historian Aino Undla phrases it (Undla 1935, 210). Suburg was familiar with the works of Immanuel Kant, John Stuart Mill and other European philosophers along with a number of books by German writers (J. W. Goethe, F. Schiller, F. Klopstock). She was familiar with the European feminist movement probably through German newspapers and tried to introduce feminist ideas through *Linda*, writing about feminist congresses and the leading European and American feminists of the time. The woman question acquired importance for Suburg because of personal experience that made her see the subjugated position of Estonian women. She has, for example, referred to the issue in her memoires The Suburg Family ("Suburgi perekond," Suburg 1924/2002) and in her autobiography My Combat with Fate ("Minu saatusega võitluskäik," Suburg 1914). Therefore, feminism became the inseparable part of Suburg's world-view according to which she shaped her approach to women issues. She thus countered the Baltic-German conservative ideology of gender according to which home was the woman's sphere of activity.

Analysing the concept of woman in *Linda*, Aino Undla-Põldmäe identifies it as the "new woman" (Undla-Põldmäe 1981, 286). A programmatic concept of the new woman was presented in the article "Emancipirt!" (1888) and carried out with "a special ideological courage and necessary sharpness" (Undla-Põldmäe 1981, 285). Emancipirt is defined as "escaped from somebody's rule; freed." What follows is the description of women's plights through history, how women came to be under the male dominance and what the consequences were for women whose mental abilities were stunted because of the lack of development possibilities. Consequently, an ideology was born that justified the lesser mental abilities and achievements of women with their biological peculiarities; namely, with the lesser weight of the female brain that does not enable women to achieve the sharpness of a male mind. On the other hand, the European women who started to "emerge from under the serfdom of men, from the obtuse and mind-killing realm" started to be called the émancipiritus. However, in order to marginalize women who have acquired education as men have and have a wish to participate in the public life, a negative connotation was created around the word émancipiritus that implied at "a breach of her nature as a woman," which Suburg contested (Suburg 1888a, 247–50).

Suburg's argumentation is very logical when she claims:

from where does a woman take those learning abilities, those gifts for skills, those powers of the mind; in a word: a whole educational hardware for the development of the mind when nature itself has not given those to her? But if nature, that is our Creator, in its greatness of mind itself has given those to women, it would constantly check that the gifts, or, in other words the possibilities would not be smothered away, but that these were used for this life, improved, increased to the level they possibly can. (Suburg 1888a, 249).

"Emancipiring" is the duty of a woman, Suburg continues, treating it as a sort of categorical imperative. Nevertheless, Suburg has to admit that Estonian women are far from the goal since "the spirit of our Estonian woman is so enslaved that she has not even started thinking about emancipation" (Suburg 1888a, 250). Estonian women first and foremost need a mental awakening and educational possibilities in order to reach the level of Finnish women. Therefore it was not necessary to scare women in Estonia with the emancipation word because this word has no power in Estonian (Suburg 1888a, 250).

The development of the "new woman" presupposed new upbringing and new education, to which Suburg dedicated a number of articles in *Linda* (Suburg 1888a, 1888b, 1888c). Education was for women the vehicle in life. Woman's education meant first and foremost a woman's mental development and not concentrating only on the development of housewife's skills. Education also meant a balance between the mind and the body, meaning that both mental as well as physical abilities needed to be developed (Suburg 1888b, 70–71, 236). Before anything else, education was needed to develop the mind, the ability to think, and not be based on memorisation, actual stuffing oneself with facts, a practice common to the teaching and learning methods of the time (Andresen 2002, 232–46). Educating women was important also because as mothers women were educating the next generation and thus influencing societal attitudes and understandings (Suburg 1888c, 80).

The concept of the "new woman" is connected to the criticism of ideology concerning gender that is based on conservative, biological determinism. By treating the understandings of femininity and masculinity, Suburg emphasised that traditional gender roles also restricted men. She showed how such traditional understandings limited the possibilities for women to be active and emphasised the discursive power of the gender ideology in oppressing women. The fear to be considered masculine did not allow women to take part in public life and express their points of view in the media (Suburg 1887a, 2–3), nor did it allow women to take up positions similarly to men (Suburg 1888a).

Suburg's "new woman" was meant to be an equal partner to the man whose self-fulfilment was carried by intellectual interests. Suburg saw women as intellectual creatures whose ability to think was similar to men, but whose personal traits—feminine balance, softness and gentility of feeling—would balance a man's masculine traits. The stress on the female intellectual abilities and aspirations differentiated Suburg's understanding of women from those common to the era. An understanding of women as a thinking creatures who were able to determine their goals in life and design their lives, was still unfamiliar in Estonia, since it was very different from the prevailing ideas of gender and from the treatment of women by the Estonian national movement. The possibility of women's free will that Suburg presupposed, and that was inseparably connected to the self-determination and educational possibilities of women, was also connected to the need to improve the legal status of women.

Suburg's concept of a "new woman" was present also in her literary output, in the story "Leeni" (1887) and "Linda, Daughter of the Nation" ("Linda, rahva tütar") (1900), where the leading female characters are portrayed as self-conscious women who demand the right to develop freely and the right to stand beside men as equal partners.

In "Leeni," Suburg introduces topics that are later covered in the articles published in *Linda*. As the author had given a literary format to her ideas, these have a broader reach: while in the articles Suburg uses firm logic of argumentation to support her ideas, in the story she creates a tangible embodiment to these ideas, a so called flesh and blood example. Leeni is ideal as a character uniting all the virtues that Suburg supposed the new woman should have: a pleasing appearance, gentle nature, intellectual abilities, and empathy towards fellow people.

Her family, first and foremost Leeni's stepmother, does not understand her aspirations and considers knowledge from books useless, seeing in a woman primarily a work slave and humble wife. Leeni's stepmother is convinced that Leeni needs to be raised into subordinate, since this is how women should be. Obeying to her stepmother, Leeni marries a man she does not love. But some years of unhappy life end in a divorce and Leeni is free to marry the man she is in love with.

The story is punctuated by Suburg's opinions and the storyteller's addresses to the reader which explicate Suburg's views on different issues concerning women, especially married women's free will and right for self-determination, or women's self-fulfilment and educational possibilities. Suburg also criticises the frame of mind common to the era that raises girls to be "toiling machines." Thus Suburg sees poor education and stupidity to be the main obstacle for the development possibilities of women. The story ends with a moral conclusion that women should not be denied the possibility to develop freely, but that the real freedom lays in the free acceptance of your responsibilities. Aino Undla has noted that this standpoint sounds very similar to Immanuel Kant's categorical imperative (Undla 1935, 209).

In the story "Linda, Daughter of the Nation" (1900), the main character is also an educated woman who, not having found use for her education, has to do hard work in a farm. She is virtuous, chaste and extremely industrious. Many important topics that Suburg has touched upon in the articles in *Linda* are interwoven into the story. According to Aino Undla, the story could be considered a philosophical novel that in its mode reminds us of Plato's dialogues:

Here the author does not tell morals, but the characters take turns in discussing the world's important questions. We can find whole articles form *Linda* coming from the lips of one or another character; the author has collected all her thoughts concerning her world view: the demand of equality with men, valuing intellectual achievements, chastity, purity, etc. (Undla 1935, 217)

By the time of its publication, the story ended up in a different socio-cultural context than Suburg's earlier literary production, and it was therefore overshadowed by other literary works such as Eduard Vilde's *To the Frozen North* ("Külmale maale") or August Kitzberg's *The Werewolf* ("Libahunt") (217).

Suburg practised and applied her ideas and understandings in her school for girls with progressive educational principles (Einasto 1969; Undla-Põld-mäe 2002, 487–90). Thus, Suburg indeed implemented the idea of a "new woman" in reality and tried, through the girls' school, to rear a new genera-tion of women who would be free from outdated gender stereotypes and who would be able to find employment outside homes.

The Reception of Suburg's Ideas

Because of their polemical nature, Suburg's views generated positive as well as negative responses. Critics feared that such ideas would undermine the tra-ditional gender system. The publication of *Linda* was received warmheartedly by Estonian newspapers such as *The Postimees* and *Olevik*, but *Tallinna Sõber* saw in *Linda* a threat to the existing social order (Undla-Põldmäe 1981, 280–281). Nevertheless, *Olevik* also found that although it is difficult to say anything about a new magazine on the basis of its first issue, a "peculiar standpoint" was visible there (Eesti ajakirjad 1888, 1887c, 1).

Tallinna Sõber, a newspaper created in order to "provide counterpropaganda and watch over the Estonian newspapers" (Undla-Põldmäe 1981, 280–281), published an article in which it called the introductory article in *Linda* "the drums of war." *Tallinna Sõber* defends traditional gender roles claiming that nature itself has determined the distribution of work according to gender, which is now being destroyed by the *Zeitgeist*. The emancipation movement that demands freedom for women and the destroying of the traditional divi-sion of labour comes from the same source. A woman needs to keep doing what she is doing; otherwise she might lose her femininity. Femininity means womanly gentility:

> To take part in literary activities has never been forbidden for a woman, but also in this she must remain within the boundaries of what is hers by nature; otherwise she may wonder why no one wants to take responsibil-ity for her writing and put money into publishing it. It is not the 'ambi-tions' of men that stand against a female starting 'working' and 'fighting' in the dusty fields of the world out there; it is rather a deeper knowledge of the 'nature of her mind' and the respect for this nature. It is 'ambi-tion' that drives some women out of the boundaries that nature itself has determined. Seeking for 'honour' and acclaim on the dusty fields of the

world does not combine well with the gentleness that is the adornment and power of women and what she has to use to keep men from brutalities and make also them defend the weaker in education. If emancipation destroyed this gentleness the world would fall into a bottomless brutality." [---] "It is the spirit of time that has left the spirituality and through that fallen into pessimism that has created this outrageous movement that is called 'liberating women' (Emancipation), but that is nothing more in its deepest of meanings than a revolt against the Word of the Lord and laws of nature, and *Linda* obviously wants to be the champion of this movement. (Uued raamatud, 1887, 2)

The *Tallinna Sõber*'s article eloquently exemplifies the gender discourse of the time, the borders within which femininity or masculinity was understood and which Suburg was criticising in her writings. But later also other newspapers adopted a more critical attitude. Criticism was countered in *Linda*'s articles that argued in defence of its viewpoints (see e.g. L.T. 1888, 148–149). Critical attitude towards *Linda* also reached Estonian literary history: in the Estonian literary history Karl August Hermann expresses an opinion that despite the educational content of *Linda*, the whole of it cannot be recommended for reading (Hermann 1898, 518).

As *Linda* was directed at Estonian readers, its ideas might have seemed quite radical in the context of the time. First and foremost, there were not enough educated Estonian (women) readers who would have understood Suburg's ideas. Suburg herself admitted the fact:

At the time when the first women's magazine *Linda* was published it had to contend with the enemies that tried to throw stones on its way at every step. *Linda* was, after all, a thorn in the side for the whole mankind, except for some of the younger ones. She was publicly derided by political newspapers and by slandering her publisher the readers were scared off. On the other hand, there was no support or cooperation for the magazine from the women for whom *Linda* was trying so hard. There were no women intellectuals and those who were educated enough hid themselves amongst the foreign nation. *Linda* was left alone to fight with the hardships until the last drop of blood. Who would wonder that She at the end slipped away to the hands of men? (Suburg 1922, 7)

The target readership was not only small, but poorly educated and had little preparation for reading and understanding such texts. Although historian Sirje Kivimäe has claimed that "the educational possibilities for Estonian girls were quite good thanks to the Baltic-German initiative" (Kivimäe 1995, 126), most peasant girls' education was limited to three years in a village school. There were few girls and women who had the chance to learn more and get a better education. Higher education available for Estonian women was quite limited in its nature; it stressed the traditional conservative gender roles and adjusted the methods and content of education according to it (see Whelan 1995). Higher education available for women was in German and its goal was to prepare women to be private tutors at homes. The quality of the education for girls did not reach the level of the education for boys since the teachers in the lower grades of the schools for girls (*Töchterschulen*) were not educated enough (Whelan 1995, 170–71). Male teachers were mostly employed in the higher grades of the schools for girls since women were not considered intellectually capable enough to master the discipline on a sufficient enough level for teaching (Whelan 1995, 171). What is more, the curriculum for the schools for girls was not comparable to that of the gymnasiums for young men, where the emphasis lay on classical disciplines. The curriculum for girls was adjusted to suit their lower intellectual abilities. The teaching of sciences, especially mathematics, was limited because there was no place in the education of women for theoretical knowledge and abstract thinking (Whelan 1995, 172).

Sirje Kivimäe considers the main reason for the low circulation of *Linda* to be its emphasis on the emancipation, independence and education of women (Kivimäe 1995, 126). Aino Undla-Põldmäe has expressed similar points of view, saying that "the ideas that Suburg expressed came too early for the Estonian readers: truth about the situation of women and about drinking" (Undla-Põldmäe 1981, 303). Suburg's views—not only about the women question, but about attitudes towards church or condemning alcoholism—expressed in a frank and direct manner (a mode of expression not expected from women), came across as sharp, causing (female) readers to withdraw. A fear for social stigmatizing also considerably influenced the amount of female readers: Suburg has described in her memoires how women did not dare to read the magazine in public (Suburg 1924/2002, 452).

Conclusion

The emancipation issue became accentuated in the second half of the nineteenth century and put emphasis on the education of women in order to create possibilities for women to get work in the modernizing society. The discussion that took place in Estonian newspapers brought forth different views on the role and position of women in society and at home. Generally speaking, these views remained confined to conservative concepts of gender relying on an understanding based on biological determinism and different gender roles. These were also reflected in the social organisation of life. Women were seen as connected to the domestic, men were seen as connected to the public sphere. Therefore, women's education was to prepare them for household chores and childcare, but only to a much lesser extent provided her with skills for positions and work outside the home. Such an understanding was becoming a part of Estonian national identity and it was supported by the leading figures of the national movement, such as Carl Robert Jakobson and Jakob Hurt.

The first Estonian feminist Lilli Suburg's attempts to disrupt the dominant discourse were reflected in her writings, published both in the magazine *Linda* as well as other Estonian media outlets. Suburg's criticism drew attention to the (lawless) status of women in society both on the level of laws and general attitudes. Suburg saw a chance in educating women and in changing gender roles and ideology that was based on biological determinism. Besides the magazine *Linda*, Suburg advocated these ideas in her literary production. Her positive programme—the idea about the "new woman"—was multifaceted covering upbringing, education and the possibilities of self-fulfilment.

According to Suburg's ideas, the emphasis on liberation posed women as individual beings and as partners equal to men with equal rights to develop her personality. Liberation consisted in giving women opportunities for better education and recognizing their right for self-determination. Women should not have an obligation to live for somebody else—household, husband, children—satisfying their needs, but they should have the right to determine their own needs and set their own goals in life. A woman had to demand more of life than keeping herself busy with everyday matters; she should develop her intellectual abilities and try to find balance between mind and body.

Suburg treated masculinity and femininity, the roles of men and women, as different but complimentary to each other. Her ideal was "equality in differences." Suburg expected a change in the male gender role, demanding men to be compassionate partners and husbands for women and good fathers for their children who take part in their upbringing.

Suburg's emancipation principles, based on enlightenment ideas, did not stop at the question of gender, but reached also the questions of morals. Suburg propagated that society needs to abandon restrictive biases regarding single unmarried women, and emphasised national liberation. Suburg's argumentation in support of her ideas was based on rational arguments and logic, refuting stereotypes of the time.

Suburg's novel ideas which were at times presented through a complicated verbal form as she was, due to German-language education, more fluent in German than in Estonian, brought besides positive also negative and polemical responses. Suburg also lacked a readership with sufficient education who would fully understand her ideas. Furthermore, there was no one in the Estonian cultural sphere, who would have been as radical and whose argumentation in gender issues would have been carried by such rational logic. Suburg simply lacked a context of like-minded thinkers and she was ahead of her time. The issue of emancipation found firmer footing in Estonia only at the beginning of the twentieth century in the context of the 1905 revolution, when the question of civil rights for women began to gain more explicit address.

References

Andresen, Lembit. 2002. *Eesti rahvakooli ja pedagoogika ajalugu, III. Koolirefor-mid ja venestamine (1803–1918)* [The history of Estonian school and peda-gogics, III. School reforms and russification (1803–1918]. Tallinn: Avita.

Annus, Endel and Tiina Loogväli. 2002. *Eestikeelne ajakirjandus 1766–1940* [Estonian journalism 1766–1940]. Vol. I. Tallinn: Eesti Akadeemiline Raamatukogu.

"Eesti emmad" [Estonian mothers]. 1863. *Perno Postimees,* June 12.

"Naesterahvas Rootsi ja Norramaal" [A woman in Sweden and Norway].1881. *Tartu Eesti Seitung,* October 28.

"Naesterahwa töödest Eesti kirjanduses" [About women's writing in Estonian literature]. 1887a. *Wirulane,* May 11.

"Naisterahvas" [A woman]. 1887b. *Virulane,* June 1, June 8, June 15.

"Eesti ajakirjad 1888" [Estonian newspapers 1888]. 1887c. *Olevik,* December 14.

"Sõnumid isamaalt" [Messages from the fatherland]. 1889. *Olevik,* June 19.

"Mõnda meie aja naesterahva liikumisest" [Some words of contemporary women's movement]. 1894. *Eesti Postimees,* December 24, December 31.

"Naesterahvas ajaloos" [A woman in history]. 1895.*Postimees,* February 20, February 21, February 23.

"Eesti naisterahvas" [Estonian woman]. 1896.*Olevik,* June 11, June 18.

Einasto, Eva. 1969. "L. Suburg pedagoogina" [L. Suburg as a pedagogue]. In *Eesti kooli ja pedagoogilise mõtte ajaloo küsimusi, I* [The questions of the history of Estonian school and pedagogical ideas, I], edited by Aleksander Elango, 41–58. Tartu: Tartu Riiklik Ülikool.

Fuchs, Rachel G., and Victoria E. Thompson. 2005. *Women in Nineteenth Cen-tury Europe.* Hampshire, New York: Palgrave Macmillan.

Hermann, Karl August. 1898. *Eesti kirjanduse ajalugu esimesest algusest meie ajani* [The history of Estonian literature from the very beginning until nowadays]. Tartu.

Jakobson, Carl Robert. 1881. "Meie tütarlaste koolitamisest" [About training of our girls]. *Sakala,* January 10.

Kivimaa, Katrin. 2009. *Rahvuslik ja modernne naiselikkus eesti kunstis 1850–2000* [A national and a modern femininity in Estonian art 1850–2000]. Tartu: Tartu Ülikooli Kirjastus.

Kivimäe, Sirje. 1995. "Esimesed naisseltsid Eestis ja nende tegelased" [First Estonian women societies and their figures]. In *Seltsid ja ühiskonna muu-tumine: talupojaühiskonnast rahvusriigini* [The societies and the social

change: from the peasant society to the nation state], edited by Ea Jansen
and Jaanus Arukaevu,118–135. Tartu, Tallinn: Eesti Ajalooarhiiv, TA Ajaloo Instituut.

"Kolm pilti" [Three images]. 1889. *Linda*, August 23.

"Kriitik" [The critic]. 1888. *Linda*, August 10.

Laar, Mart. 2006. *Äratajad* [Awakers]. Tallinn: Grenader.

L. T. [= The Editor of Linda]. 1888. "Kõiki auusaid..." [All honest....]. *Linda*,
April 9.

L. T. [= The Editor of Linda]. 1889. "Omalt poolt peame..." [We have to ...]
Linda, May 30.

Lukas, Liina. 2004. *"New Women* baltisaksa kirjanduses" [New Women in Baltic German literature]. *Ariadne Lõng* 1/2:150–171.

Mattheus, Ave. 2008. "Soospetsiifilise eesti laste- ja noortekirjanduse lätetel:
Carl Robert Jakobsoni tütarlastelugemik *Helmed*" [The gendered sources of
Estonian children's literature: a reader for girls The beads]. *Ariadne Lõng*
1/2: 94–115.

P. P. 1879. "Mõned tähtsad ütelused naisterahva koolitamise ja kasvatamise
kohta" [Some important claims about the schooling and educating of
women]. *Sakala*, February 24.

Simberg, A. 1887. "Meie naisterahwa küsimus" [The question of our women].
Eesti Postimees, February 28, March 6, March 14, March 21.

Sirk, Väino. 2011. "Rahvakoolisüsteemi institutsionaalsed probleemid
ärkamisaja eesti mõtteloos (1860.–1880. aastad)" [Institutional problems
of folk schools in the Estonian ideology of the national awakening era
(between the 1860s and mid-1880s). *Acta Historica Tallinnensia* 16: 86–108.

Suburg, Lilli. 1887a. "Sõnakene suguõdedele" [A word to women]. *Linda*,
October 15.

———. 1887b. "Paarrahvas ja üksikud" [Married couples and singles]. *Linda*,
November 15, December 28.

———. 1887c. "Leeni, ehk igavene käsualune" [Leeni or the eternal under-
ling]. *Linda*, October 15, November 15, December 28.

———. 1888a. "Emancipirt!" [Emancipated!]. *Linda*, July 15.

Suburg, Lilli. 1888b. "Kodu ja Kool" [Home and school]. *Linda*, February 15,
May 20.

———. 1888c. "Mis piavad meie nüidse aja Eesti naisterahva püidmised olema"
[Which have to be the ambitions of our contemporary Estonian women].
Linda, March 15, April 9.

———. 1888d. "Viimane seletus "Oleviku" nooriku Kai Supp'ile" [The last explanation to young woman Kai Supp from Olevik]. *Linda*, August 10.

———. 1889a. "Naisterahvaste õiiguste suurendamine meie Läänekuber-manngudes" [About expanding the rights of women in our West provinces]. *Linda*, July 15.

———. 1889b. "Uuema aja paariminemised" [Contemporary marriages]. *Linda*, July 15.

———. 1890. "Sõbralised juhatused noorde inimestele. Meheleminemisest" [Friendly guides to young people. About marriage]. *Linda*, March 24.

———. 1891. "Abielu" [Marriage]. *Linda*, March 23.

———. 1914. "Minu saatusega võitluskäik" [My struggle with destiny]. *Naisterahwa Töö ja Elu*, May 28, June 25, July 30, August 27, September 24.

———. 1922. "Eesti naistele" [To Estonian women]. *Postimees*, July 15.

———. 1924/2002. "Suburgi perekonna elulugu" [The life story of the Suburg family]. In Lilli Suburg, *Kogutud kirjatööd* [Selected works], edited by Aino Undla-Põldmäe, 313–459. Tallinn: Eesti Raamat.

———. 2008. "Päevikukatkeid" [The fragments of the diary]. *Ariadne Lõng* 1/2: 148–150.

Tamul, Sirje. 1999. "Saateks" [Introduction]. In *Vita Academica, Vita Feminea*, edited by Sirje Tamul, 9-20. Tartu: Tartu Ülikooli Kirjastus.

-ts.[=Hindrik Prants]. 1892. "Naesterahva küsimusest" [About woman's question]. *Postimees*, April 22.

Undla, Aino. 1935. Esimesed eesti naiskirjanikud, nende kujunemine, anded ja ideaalid [First Estonian women writers, their development, talents, and ideals]. EKLA [=Estonian Cultural History Archives], reg. 1992/70.

Undla-Põldmäe, Aino. 1981. "Lilli Suburg ja tema ajakiri 'Linda'" [Lilli Suburg and her magazine Linda]. In *Koidulauliku valgel: uurimusi ja artikleid* [Under the light of the dawn-singer], 277–304. Tallinn: Eesti Raamat.

Undla-Põldmäe, Aino. 2002. "Lilli Suburgi tütarlastekool" [Lilli Suburg's school for girls]. In Lilli Suburg, *Kogutud kirjatööd* [Selected works], edited by Aino Undla-Põldmäe, 481–491. Tallinn: Eesti Raamat.

"Uued raamatud" [New books]. 1887. *Tallinna Sõber*, December12.

Veiderma, Aleksander. 2000. *Elu hariduse radadel* [The life on the roads of education]. Tallinn: Eesti Keele Sihtasutus.

Whelan, Heide. 1995. "The Debate on Women's Education in the Baltic Provinces, 1850–1905." In *Bevölkerungsverschiebungen und Socialer Wandel in den Baltischen Provinzen Russlands 1850–1914*, edited by Gert von Pistohlkors,

Andreis Plakans, Paul Kaegbein, 163–180. Lüneburg: Institut Nordost-
deutsches Kulturwerk.

————. 1999. *Adapting to Modernity. Family, Caste and Capitalism among the Baltic
German Nobility.* Köln, Weimar, Wien: Böhlau Verlag.

-W. 1880. "Naisterahvas" [A woman]. *Sakala*, May 3, May 10, May 17, May 24.

Literary Knowledge in Historical Study
The Case of Josef Škvorecký's *The Engineer of Human Souls*

Kalle Pihlainen*

Abstract

The article examines the possibility of "literary knowledge" in historical research from the point of view of respecting the autonomy of the literary work. Conventionally, historical studies tend to approach literary texts much like any other sources, asking what it is that those sources might reveal or express about the context of their conception. Although this is an entirely legitimate question from the point of view of history, it can easily lead to reductive readings of the works at hand. Using Josef Škvorecký's novel *The Engineer of Human Souls* as a case study, the article attempts to elaborate on ways of reading that take the complexity and literary meaning-making processes of texts seriously—and thus refuse to reduce literary artworks to reflections of a context already pre-figured by historical knowledge. Such readings can proceed, it is argued, only by a careful tracing outward of significance and broader context from the references and meaning-construction operative within texts.

Introduction

The relationship of a literary text to the literary tradition, as well as to broader cultural dialogue, is often seen as problematic—at least when it is not unreflectively taken for granted, as so often seems to be the case in historical study. Importantly, the cultural context has significance for the study of literature only if we assume that social situations impact on an artwork and that art can have a broader effect on society. Sensible assumptions, it would seem. The interesting question, then, is that of how literature can be approached in relation to surrounding culture without merely reducing the relation to some kind of reflection. My aim here is to illustrate how the historicity of a (literary) text—its situatedness in time and space—may be approached primarily from the text itself, thus making traditional questions of source criticism secondary issues in the use of literary texts—even by historians.

* Kalle Pihlainen is an Academy of Finland Research Fellow working on the theory and philosophy of history in the Department of Philosophy at Åbo Akademi University.

My examination replicates the duality of the title. Primary interest is in the dialogue between literary texts within the discourse of literature as well as in the ways in which such literary discourse relates to the real world and thus, by extension, also to historical study. In order not to forget the point of view of practical historical research and writing, I will focus on specific material. The case chosen is that of the novel *The Engineer of Human Souls* (published in Czech in 1977 [hereafter EOHS]) by Josef Škvorecký, a Czech emigrant to Canada.

As my intention is first and foremost to present an argument in defence of a particular sensibility for the use of literary texts in historical study, I will not seek a comprehensive reading of the novel but instead approach it in terms of a single structuring question: what is its relation to Western ideas of realism, reason and rationality (the same ideas that undergird the fundamental definitions of conventional historical study)? Although the novel could be tackled via other questions it is, in my reading, the problem of rationality that offers the best opportunities for locating its inner or internal historicity. Clearly, *The Engineer of Human Souls* is the product of a particular intellectual moment, a moment that also crystallizes the problems of modernist thought. Which relates also to my main reason for choosing this novel: it demonstrates a great deal of self-consciousness regarding the problems typical to its genre (which is in fact a characteristic of many if not most modernist literary texts). Along with that self-consciousness comes an ironic attitude to literary study and the interpretation of human actions in general. The text thus offers, I think, a perfect opportunity for a theory of history discussion; in so doing, it is also an important reminder that every text needs to participate in its "unravelling"— it needs to originate and justify the route that a reading takes.

Before proceeding with a reading, a number of further "contextualizing" and qualifying remarks are in order: *The Engineer of Human Souls* is more closely connected to a North American literary tradition than a Czech context. The demonic, supernatural aspect associated with Prague literature, for example, is largely missing from the work. Suggestively, J. P. Stern (1992, 68) has proposed that such a demonic dimension most often results from the absence of a strong literary tradition.[1] A parallel point has also been made by George Steiner who—in a study on the particularity of the Russian novel—

---

1 Speaking of the supernatural in Prague literature, Stern also mentions Edgar Allan Poe, whose works are repeatedly referenced in *The Engineer of Human Souls*. Stern has it that, in general: "This leaning towards the demonic is characteristic of a literature which ... lacked the social *données* of European Realism" (Stern 1992, 68).

shows how geographical distance easily leads to the transgression of traditional boundaries (Steiner 1959, 35 and 42–43).[2]
I would claim that this is an important insight with respect to emigrant
authors as well, even though the distance there is as much mental (to the
customs of a "new land") as it is geographical (from the "homeland" and its
traditions). In my analysis, I also assume that the relationship of emigrant
writers to the literary discourse is exceptional: as a result of the traditional
restrictions in the old country and the strangeness of the new, (often per-
sistently) foreign customs, innovation and the traditions of the new land
become objects of particular appreciation. In *The Engineer of Human Souls*,
this is evident through a strong internalization and deployment of the Eng-
lish-language literary tradition.
Because *The Engineer of Human Souls* appears to be highly autobiographical,
there is a temptation to identify its author, the writer, publisher and literature
professor Josef Škvorecký, with the main character in the book, the author
and literature professor Daniel Smiricky. For this reason too, the work offers
a good opportunity to consider how literature might be used by historians
without simply comparing the contents presented with the historical and biographical details of the author's life. The basic premise in my analysis is that
the "other"—the foreign subject that the reader is introduced to by the text—
is Smiricky, not Škvorecký. In this way the work also becomes a useful test case
for the kinds of theories concerning the reading of literary texts that I lean on
here.
At points I will examine the ideas present in *The Engineer of Human Souls*
also for their theoretical content as noted. This is because, as I will sketch
out, they are intimately linked to mainstream literary theory and research,
particularly that of the novel's writing time. In formulating my theoretical
position, I naturally draw on a range of other quite diverse sources too. At the
core of my approach is the Anglo-Saxon history of ideas or intellectual history tradition to which—at least when broadly understood—the bulk of my
sources belong: Isaiah Berlin, George Steiner, J. P. Stern, Hayden White and
Dominick LaCapra. In the essay "The Context in the Text: Method and Ideology in Intellectual History," Hayden White explores what at the time at least
were new possibilities for study in the history of ideas (White 1987, 185–213).
These are possibilities I think still need to be considered. Along with LaCapra's book *History, Politics and the Novel*, that essay provides the core theoreti-

2 According to Steiner, this is equally the case with early American authors. He mentions Hawthorne,
for instance, whose presence is also strong in *The Engineer of Human Souls*.

cal starting point for me here. As is well known, both White and LaCapra also pay particular attention to the narrative similarities between literature and histories.

On the Possibility of Literary Knowledge

The nature of the relationship between structures and individual agency constitutes a major problem in the humanities. This same problem is central in examinations of the relation of the literary text to the real world. To exaggerate: we must choose whether literature simply reflects material reality or whether the creative writer acts in some way free of the environment. As Alan Swingewood says of the literary text as societal document:

> Sociological themes, elements and problems, may be extracted from a literary text, for example, and related to similar processes in society; different kinds of hero can be linked with changes in social and political organisation; broad artistic movements, such as expressionism, realism and modernism can be read as reflections of historical development. (Swingewood 1986, 3)

In an analysis focused on the referentiality or representational nature of literature, the claim might simply be that the protagonist of *The Engineer of Human Souls*, Daniel Smiricky, stands as a symbol of the historical shift from a modernist worldview (the bright-eyed and idealistic youth) to a postmodern one (the sceptical intellectual). Such an approach is useful—particularly in traditional history of ideas studies—because it facilitates the process of classification that most often is the goal. It gives a good overview of the general tone of the text, of its "guiding ideology" as it were. However, this leads to the simplification of any given text, leading to blindness for its individuality and nuances.

If we are to believe the narrator and main character of *The Engineer of Humans Souls*, literature professor Daniel Smiricky, "Art captures that essence which reality, sometimes more, sometimes less, spreads thin. In art, the essence presents itself as an undiluted, powerful possibility. And because art incarnates what is possible, it can mean anything under the sun" (EOHS 549).[3] According to Smiricky, then, art describes reality as it could be, not as

---

3 The question of the limits of art and entertainment is notoriously complex, and I will not attempt to deal with it here. Suffice it to say that these dimensions are not mutually exclusive. In being the extremely self-conscious novel that it is, *The Engineer of Human Souls* notes this problem in its subtitle:

it is. In a study of the relation of fictive and possible worlds in literary texts, Ruth Ronen (1994, 10–11) substantiates this idea, arguing that fictionality should not be defined simply in terms of a departure from reality. Instead, one must recognize that the relation between the fictional and the real is always pragmatically and generically determined; the intuition that untruths could constitute a definition of fictionality is insufficient. (Nonetheless, I would say there is a crucial dissimilarity to be noted between fictional and possible worlds: although a possible world can constitute an internally coherent whole just as do fictional ones, examination of it requires a point of comparison in the actual world. This distinction is particularly illuminating and central to a consideration of the relation of the literary work and its historical context.)

This same view is shared by Hayden White, who—in a foreword to Jacques Rancière's *The Names of History*—suggests that truthfulness is not the key issue but that "truth" follows the forms of expression that a particular discourse is devoted to (White 1994, xvii). In other words, a fictional world should not be examined through the actual one, but as an autonomous entity. The literary work needs to be seen for what it is: first and foremost an independent and self-contained system of references. From this it follows that "literary knowledge" needs to have a different function in historical research than the document.

From the point of view of a work's autonomy, it is necessary to think of literary knowledge as something other than referential—in subordinating the work's artistic dimension to the functional we run the risk of losing its significance and will end up seeing only the random and fragmented picture that it happens to reflect of the actual world at the time of its creation. For conventionally oriented historical studies at least, the recognition of "worklikeness" is problematic, however, because it begs the question of what some autonomous and largely self-referencing literary knowledge could tell us about the real world.

It might be preferable to think that the historian's task is not to determine what factual data a work can supply concerning the world of its inception but rather to show which ideas in the work stand in meaningful relation to reality. In his ironic style, Smiricky, the protagonist of the novel, defends the same idea, describing how much he suffers for literature students whose teacher focuses only on literary issues—the teacher "who, lecturing on the function

---

An Entertainment on the Old Themes of Life, Women, Fate, Dreams, the Working Class, Secret Agents, Love and Death.

of colour in *The Scarlet Letter*, deals only with the function of colour in *The Scarlet Letter*" (EOHS 64). It is, instead, important to see both a work's artistic nature *and* its integral relation to society, history and human aspirations.

The primary function of a literary text may, I think, justifiable be said to be poetic. Hence such a text's referentiality is also directed firstly towards the discourse of fiction and it would be unreasonable to claim that this would somehow change when we treat it as a source for historical research. Since my intention here is to show how literary texts can be used for historical research, however, the question of what a literary work can reveal of its context still needs to be asked. What, exactly, might literary knowledge be?

Once we reject the idea that the literary product simply reflects reality, the question of how such a thing can be produced becomes central: *how are ideas transported from reality to a literary work?* Conceptually, it is possible to distinguish a number of levels in this process: the linguistic representation of non-linguistic material; "artistic decisions" dictated by literary conventions; tangible limitations (strong public opinion about a particular matter, for example); and ideological decisions. Although these are interdependent in complex ways, they can—continuing to simplify and exaggerate a little—be seen to correspond with language, literary discourse, the social situation, and the individual's perspective.

What seems clear is that the literary text, precisely because it is a text, follows the conditions of its own materiality. As far as language is concerned, it is sufficient to note that each text reflects its context through the linguistic "constellation" it employs, the linguistic conventions it makes use of. This has, of course, a strong impact on other aspects of the text, the text's worldview and its ideological emphases. Most important, however, is the *content* of the text. As Smiricky states, "for even the most basic linguistic efforts one must have something to say" (EOHS 555).

On a general level, fictive expression is completely dependent not only on language but also on the prevailing ideologies of a society, yet presented in such a way that none of these ideologies dominates the others.[4] The question of the superiority of any particular ideology ultimately depends also on the author's goals or at least on his or her worldview. Studying a particular indi-

---

4 The background to this claim is in Mikhail Bakhtin's now-familiar idea of the polyphonic novel, a novel that is not controlled by one (usually the author's) worldview. Instead, such works present a number of conflicting voices, of which the author's is one among many. The possibility for such opposing views makes for a novel in which there is no clear ending. Issues are not resolved to the satisfaction of a single worldview but cultural dialogue continues instead, just as it does in reality (Bakhtin 1991, 50–57 and 127–138).

vidual or their writings historically is thus always also a study of the society, a matter of locating the individual in the collective practices of his or her time.

In further elaborating his position on these issues, Swingewood makes use of Lucien Goldmann's idea of an active, productive subject who endows the text with a clear identity and a unified worldview. Through this kind of idea, the issue of the transposition of collective values and beliefs to literary products appears more straightforward. According to Swingewood (1986, 27), Goldmann's collective subjects manifest an ideologically shaped consciousness divorced from reality. They also have the potential to reach a form of awareness that is in direct contact with reality. This is what Goldmann terms a potential consciousness. Much as in Theodor Adorno's aesthetic theory, also in Goldmann's view it is exceptional individuals—artists and philosophers— who can realize this potential. This realization is not, however, the realization of the individual's potential as such but rather, Goldmann claims, these people succeed in formulating a profound expression of the consciousness of the social group that they represent. Understood thus, one might also say that the author gives the ideological valuations and desires of his or her community or class a chance to live on in the work. (It should be noted that at stake are not only—or even primarily—those valuations and preferences that the author is conscious of, however. Here, too, it is a matter of the frame of reference created by the community, of the "tools" that define the opportunities for thought.)

The collective consciousness to be discovered in *The Engineer of Human Souls* is not, as far as I am able to see, primarily that of the Canadian emigrant community it describes. Rather, it is that of a set of literary and historically aware intellectuals with shared, and potentially postmodernist, sensibilities. Postulating a collective consciousness is a problematic idea, and it is especially so perhaps for emigrants because of the nature of their common denominator. Smiricky describes their heterogeneity well:

... generations of emigrants layered upon one another, thrown fortuitously together by the unfortunate course of events in a distant land. Pauperized, re-established, industrious, hungry for money, sentimental, hungry for freedom, limited, intellectual, mean, merciful. All kinds. (EOHS 243)

A familiality of sensibilities among a group of intellectuals seems an easier thing to show, however. Not (I would say) by coincidence, Derrida's *De la gram-*

matologie (1967) was translated into English a year before the publication of *The Engineer of Human Souls*. A case can be made for a particular historical situation that presents itself in the affinities of the texts produced by a community, as an image of its collective consciousness. As Hayden White says, the ideas presented in a text set the reader in that *literary* world in which the text was written. The world that a work constructs relates to the real world through other texts (White 1987, 205; this is of course a very Derridean view as well). In *The Engineer of Human Souls* this is obvious through the abundance of direct and indirect literary references. By following these references, the work can be read in relation to a broader context. Importantly, this broader context cannot (read: should not) be accessed without such reference. At stake is the context *in the text*, after all.

In my view, a key ideological change that *The Engineer of Human Souls* marks is the cultural crisis of intellectuals that can be said to have begun in the spring of 1968, especially with the events in Paris. Derrida's ideas of the crisis of Western rationality are closely tied to this change in the cultural status of intellectuals, a change that is also perceivable in the ironic and questioning tone of *The Engineer of Human Souls*. Although the work is not in any way categorical on this, the same collective ideology certainly plays a central role.

Historical Events as Literary Knowledge

Drawing on Paul Ricoeur, we can say that plot places us at the juncture of temporality and narrativity (Ricoeur 1984; White 1987, 51). In order to be historical, an event has to be something more than a singular, contingent phenomenon. It needs to be emplotted along with other events, and its place in a narrative cannot be arbitrary (see White 1987, 51). In other words, we cannot for instance claim that the French Revolution occurred before the American Revolution. Presented in this way, this is, of course, self-evident, but the justification for emphasizing it becomes clear when we combine it with the problem of the "truthfulness" of literature. The most obvious difference between literary and historical knowledge comes to involve the relation of these discursive modes to the actual world. In practice, this is really only to say that literary texts can present things invented (the content of a literary text does not need to have a factual relationship with reality) while history writing is more clearly tied to historical facts. For historians to make use of fiction they need to view it historically. This means being attentive to the historicity of the text, ultimately its situatedness in time and space.

But there are at least two ways of approaching the historicity of literary texts. We can search for the historical facts present in a text and, following a fairly standard historical approach, examine their value in terms of "truthfulness." This can be done by weighing their probative value through traditional source criticism: by assessing the reliability of the source through questions of the author's purpose and so on, as well as by comparing it to other similar sources. Choosing this option denies the work the kind of autonomy that I have advocated here. Another option is to look at the work as a sign of its time of writing. What should be understood, however, is that even though this already shifts the focus from the truth-value of the text's content to its form and its "message" (or one could also say ideological content), the text still needs to be treated as an independent artwork before even this alternative can do justice to it *as a whole*. Reading a text as a manifesto or message about its time is just as reductive of its complexity as viewing it as a reflection of its context. More sensitivity is to me needed regarding the constructed and object-nature of literary texts; their complex textuality, as such.

In an exemplary analysis of Virginia Woolf's *To the Lighthouse*, Dominick LaCapra (1987, 139) distinguishes two temporal levels in the novel, arguing that the feeling of timelessness created by a text is always the result of rehearsing the past, of speaking about earlier events. This is also the case in *The Engineer of Human Souls*, where Smiricky/the narrator is constantly in the present. On this level, the internal historicity of the text is generated by the reminiscences that Smiricky engages in, giving the reader a picture of his past and hence also of his location in readers' views of history. These "journeys" are timeless, however, as Smiricky notes, in the sense that any return is only ever an illusion: "No man can step into the same river twice" (EOHS 533). Returning takes place only through means of remembering.

Without such temporal reference points within the text, however, it seems unlikely that we could tackle a work's historicity; without, that is, attempting to link it directly to reality and to our own time, in which case our views of the actual past would furnish the chance for making comparisons. That would once again, however, lead to treating the text as an unfairly one-dimensional document. *When a text is approached as a literary artwork, its historicity needs to be discovered starting from its own world.*[5]

---

5 I want to emphasize that the idea of *the text*'s inner historicity should not be understood as being about the text in some way merely identifying its place in a historical interpretation of the past or, even, providing a historical *interpretation* of its own. Rather, in question is—as with respecting the autonomy of the text more broadly—the reading of a text in such a way that its textual meaning ("the content of the form") is properly charted. White appears to this day to be most often mistakenly thought of simply as a formalist and mired in the idea of tropes. This despite everything that he has

LaCapra continues his argument by claiming that the second temporal level in the text commonly contains those events that we take to be historical, such as death and war. For him these are historical because they involve change; and hence they also act as breaking points in the narrative (LaCapra 1987, 139). I do not fully accept LaCapra's position as it seems to me that even something as uneventful as a sense of timelessness, for example, still functions as a point of comparison by which a particular state (of anticipation, expectations, change, and so on) is textually constructed and can be measured. However, despite these reservations, LaCapra's distinction is useful as it leads him to claim that the latter kind of sudden change is often set in the background (or even placed in parentheses, as it were) in literary works. In *The Engineer of Human Souls* this is most obvious at a point that might also be located using a different strategy (a point that I will thus come to somewhat circuitously):

In his analysis of Henry Adams' autobiography, White suggests that the structure of a text can be seen as an important part of its ideological content (White 1987, 204). The same idea can be found already in Lucien Goldmann, whose originality lies (according to Alan Swingewood) especially in the distinction that he makes between content and structure (form). Works can have the same content but still take on different forms. The content tells us of society and its history, whereas the structure points to the impact of reality on the genesis of the artwork, identifying those expressive or discursive strategies that provide coherence and meaning for literary texts as well as for social groups (see Swingewood 1986, 31). White also makes this point. White stresses that the task when studying a text is to determine the relations between opposing codes and to attempt to discover their hierarchy. This makes it possible, he argues, to find the explanatory model that provides the best fit. The most important clues are to be found in the structure (White 1987, 202).

At least in the case of *The Engineer of Human Souls*, such attention to structure offers an excellent starting point since the various levels of the story appear almost as still images of different periods in a life whose variedness the nar-

---

written since the late 1970s. I find surprising the fact that his idea of "the context in the text" (that serves as my inspiration here) has been so broadly overlooked. My reasons for preferring White's approach to that of Quentin Skinner, for instance, and particularly with respect to literary texts, is that White has far more literary theory sensitivity for the complexity/autonomy of such texts. One might summarize this difference by saying that White does not aim to "contextualize" but instead to find textual reasons for finding some aspects of a context meaningful. For a discussion of White and Skinner together, see Jay (2013).

rator repeatedly emphasizes. The narrator describes himself as a young man in German-occupied Czechoslovakia during the Second World War and then later as an emigrant in Canada in the 1970s. The events in between are dealt with solely through means of letters that the narrator has received and several analepses or "flashbacks." The narrator's perspective remains firmly embedded in the text's present, in the years 1976 and 1977.

From the point of view of a conventional structural analysis, the work can be said to contain two separate stories. Centrally, for the ideological message that the work presents, it is important to note that the text does not depict the transition from one system to another (or, due to the sharp distinction between them, one might even say from one story to another). The chief structural element that really connects the life of the Czech youth with that of the emigrant professor living in Canada—in addition to the narrator's subjectivity—is one short sentence: "I remember Paris in 1968" (EOHS 533). The escape (via Paris) during the Prague occupation is presented so fleetingly. Yet the sentence also makes a broader connection to the times: it reminds us that the work is also silent about the student riots in Europe and about the decline in the status of intellectuals. The function of this deliberate omission is to highlight the antagonism and contrast between the old system and the new one; the juxtaposition would suffer if the transition were explained. In my view, the omission needs to read as deliberate since the text itself points it out. Omissions that readers notice from the basis of their historical knowledge alone are not significant.

The glossing of such significant events with a single sentence seems in line with LaCapra's idea of setting them in parentheses. However, its significance needs to be explained not in terms of some kind of trauma or anxiety, but as a presentational strategy. As White (1987, 205) asserts: "to explain or interpret a rupture in a text by referring it to a rupture in the author's psyche is merely to double the problem and pass off this doubling operation as a solution to it." The structural function of a gap in the text needs to be determined.

Example Analysis: Josef Škvorecký's
Engineer of Human Souls and the Ideal of Rationality

The Engineer of Human Souls begins by presenting six quotations from the Western literary canon, which can be taken to paint a roadmap for its reading.[6]

---

6 The novel's relation to the literary tradition is a complex and interesting issue, but any systematic treatment remains beyond the reach of my analysis here. I will, however, try to deal with (inter)textual references when they link in directly with the question of the idealization of rationality.

Although White's advice is that a structural analysis should begin at the very beginning (White 1987, 196–197), I will leave the title and the overall structure for later and instead begin by examining the initial reference to William Blake. The quote is—particularly in light of the ideological rift that I have sketched out above—an obvious key to the text: "To Generalize is to be an idiot. To Particularize is the Alone Distinction of Merit. General Knowledges are those Knowledges that Idiots possess." The self-conscious and ironic tone of *The Engineer of Human Souls* is set here already since—removed from their context—Blake's statements are nothing more than a great generalization themselves.

Although not noted by the work, many readers will know that the quote comes from Blake's "art-political" work. It is a direct response to an addendum to Sir Joshua Reynolds' *Discourses*, commenting on Reynolds' ability to abstract things: "He was a great generalizer… But this disposition to abstractions, to generalizing and classification, is the great glory of the human mind…" (Blake 1976, 451)

Certainly *The Engineer of Humans Souls* demonstrates an awareness of this context: The paradox within the original excerpt from Blake is emphasized in *The Engineer of Human Souls* when it is presented completely severed from its original context, almost as a general law. But placing the quotation as a road sign at the beginning of the work is a clear comment on the issue of rationality in another way too: Even though Blake is typically defined as a representative of romanticism, he was situated temporally at a rare position between rationalism and romanticism, and his work is even more adamantly opposed to the dominance of reason and rationality than that of most other romantics.[7]

Deploying the idea of logocentrism

Blake offers an interesting starting point also with respect to the literal meaning of logocentrism. In his *Of Grammatology* (1976), Derrida defines Western thought as a search for some centring idea or theory. This he calls logocentrism—a focus on "logos" or words. In logocentric thought all meaning and content is, he argues, assumed to be present in words: reality is expected to be explainable. With certain reservations, Derrida criticizes this urge for centring and overdetermination—the hypotaxis characteristic to modernity—as limiting (Derrida 1976, passim, esp. 35). The strong desire to account for

---

7 Martin K. Nurmi (1975, 11–12), for example, situates Blake's oeuvre into the overall romantic framework, yet he too points out that it is at times quite extreme even for this.

everything rationally as well as the related attempts to construct over-arching theories, discover general laws, establish firm grounds, and create grand narratives can be argued to be based on a fear of the unexplainable—a fear of undecidability.

Within the Western literary canon, Blake is one of the earliest to have thoroughly questioned this rationalizing tendency.[8] Indeed, even with his peculiar illustrated writing—which is emblematic of all his work—he systematically denies a literal "*logos*-centrism." He also rejects the possibility of categorical explanations of the world through his mystical and sometimes also mystifying views of the spirit world. Hence it seems fair to argue that the references to Blake in *The Engineer of Human Souls* by themselves already justify the question of the work's relation to logocentrism.

Despite the much longer tradition, the denial of logocentrism needs, however, here be viewed first and foremost as part of the broader questioning of the explainability of human actions which has become increasingly widespread since the events of 1968. Obviously acutely aware of developments within literature and literary studies, Smiricky presents a number of ideas that bind him to this overall "spirit" of the time—that situate him as part of the collective consciousness affected by such thinking. To me, he sums up the futility of searching for rational explanations well with a single epigrammatic statement: "Meaning is a compulsive neurosis" (EOHS 534).

With statements like "I had again succumbed to my foolish but probably irrepressible desire to explain the inexplicable" (EOHS 5), however, Smiricky also admits that the goal of inclusive explanation presents a great temptation even for the most well-informed of scepticist intellectuals. The issue of logocentrism is central to the work, then, simply with respect to this idea of explaining. However, again in a Derridean vein, Smiricky also muses on the possible Westernness of the phenomenon:

The closely watched pedagogues of Europe do not allow their charges to err. Where would I lead them were I an Eastern pedagogue?... Perhaps the intensity of this quest for something that no one can ever find because it does not exist is the same in all ages and all systems. Fortunately most people soon lose interest in finding an answer. (EOHS 130)

---

8 In the same text that the quote comes from, Blake also claims that "Demonstration, Similitude & Harmony are Objects of Reasoning. Invention, Identity & Melody are Objects of Intuition" (Blake 1976, 474).

Smiricky's ironic attitude is strongest precisely with regard to the issue of truth. He points out his own historicity by granting that he has adopted this scepticism over the course of many years. However, he also says that he has become accustomed to the idea that even though we can indeed see every-thing in alternative ways, ultimate truth remains unsurpassed: "the primal, the real meaning, the concrete reality, is ultimately the best" (EOHS 31). White (1987, 203) is willing, as I am here, to consign such contradictory utter-ances to the peripheries of ideological content as a reflection of the diversity and complexity of reality, something that can never be completely excluded. This seems to be a justified strategy also in reading *The Engineer of Human Souls* because—even though the idea of polyphony is integral to this kind of modernist, self-conscious novel—the structure and the (inter)textual refer-ences of the text direct its reading in a well-defined direction. It might even be argued that texts that offer none of this internal historicity and variation do not support reading in terms of any literary or narrative knowledge but only as synchronic and straightforward ideological pronouncements.

Belief in progress
The Engineer of Human Souls clearly contains a strong dimension of social cri-tique. As already outlined, the objects of its critique primarily involve such acts, thoughts and beliefs based on a faith in the superiority of reason. Criti-cism of logocentrism in the work is to be expected, of course, since the repres-sion present in the totalitarian regime it describes is justified "scientifically" and this naturally sets itself up against folklore and superstition, worldviews that it attempts to replace. Indeed, a key feature of the scientific explana-tion of society is the idea of historical necessity. Even when this is not openly disclosed, it is implicit in the idea of scientific truth, the search for one cor-rect explanatory model; if everything can be rationally explained, it can also be predicted and is, in that sense, determinate (see, e.g., Isaiah Berlin 1955, 14–19). Here, this prompts questions about the relationship between a vulgar-ized Marxist historical determinism and the worldview of the novel.

In *The Engineer of Human Souls*, questioning the ideal of historical progress plays an important role. The ways in which it is tackled vary from direct ideo-logical expressions ("I do not entertain a scientific world view," EOHS 131) to ironic, apparent approval: "I usher her in, admiring her slender back and well-proportioned little bottom as she slips past. Progress does exist after all. In my parents' generation, forty-year-old women were usually three times that wide" (EOHS 177).

Smiricky's youthful text about evolution is a similarly ironic comment on historical evolution and teleological ideas of history:

> In the struggle for survival man's brain has grown, giving him an undisputed advantage, but once again this growth has not stopped at the point of maximum advantage. His rational abilities have grown, while his emotional and volitional capacities have remained unchanged. Thanks to this hypertrophy of the rational part of the brain, reality has become more and more complicated, leading to increasingly irresolvable conflicts of the reason with the emotions and the will, in turn producing individuals incapable of action—which can only be the product of the instrumental, not the reflective intelligence. Such individuals are no longer able to deal with life. Their numbers are increasing. (EOHS 138)

For my purpose here, it is noteworthy that this idea too primarily targets faith placed in reason rather than in human opportunities and capacity more generally. It is, however, located in memories, in Smiricky's youth, and thus helps alleviate the (ideological) dichotomy existing in the work. The comment seeks to show that very similar ways of thinking are—depending on the individual's tendencies—possible even within quite opposing systems. "Freedom" is not as important for thought as the opposition between systems suggests:

> Perhaps the second revolution [1968] is just a counter-revolution; perhaps it is a good thing to replace freedom with police order, which over time transforms bureaucratic decrees into natural laws in human consciousness... Perhaps clinging to freedom is really no more than an atavism after all, even the uncompromising clinging to artistic freedom... Greatness of talent is often inversely proportional to the stridency of the demands of freedom. (EOHS 323)

The similarity of the extremes of both totalitarian and capitalist systems is highlighted when Smiricky points out clearly comparable opportunities for individual action despite the tremendous ideological and structural differences. Simultaneously, the juxtaposition of systems is particularly interesting from the point of view of the expectations set by Smiricky's biographical context.

It seems quite natural that an emigrant writer would criticize the system that has been left behind.[9] Yet Smiricky's commitments to both of the two rival systems are surprisingly conflicted. Much of his critique is directed also at his new surroundings and its peculiarities. As noted, however, the bulk of the critique presented by *The Engineer of Human Souls* targets the foundation of both systems—faith in the power of reason.

In short, *The Engineer of Human Souls* draws attention to how the overemphasis of rationality is characteristic to both (effectively diametrically opposed) political and economic systems. The work does not restrict itself only to purely negative views of rationality, however, but also—in a polyphonic manner—includes different takes on the issue, depending on the particular situation and context. This diversity of opinions is one of the factors that I think justifies reading the work in relation to postmodern thought and especially to the critique of logocentrism. Irony is an integral part of this approach.

The functions of irony and the absurd

I use irony here—quite straightforwardly—to refer to a form of expression that simultaneously builds and questions the statements or beliefs that it presents. This form is characteristic of Smiricky in *The Engineer of Human Souls*. Generally, it might be said that ironic expression marks an ambivalent attitude towards considerations of reason and rationality. It reveals that the speaker is aware of the ambiguity of things and of the constructed nature of meaning. By absurdity, on the other hand, I mean the occurrence of irony in a much simpler form: Everything that appears to be contrary to reason and "common sense" can be classed as absurd. From this perspective, it is clear that irony and the absurd also constantly question each other.

A central function of irony in *The Engineer of Human Souls* appears to be that of demonstrating the reality of the things and events described—their veracity. As already mentioned, the (literary and structural) purpose of presenting contradictory content is to suggest historical change, the temporal situatedness of ideas. The same can be said to be true with regard to the function of irony: irony is necessary to provide a reference point for ideas occurring in the work. If the work did not at least partly call into question its overt message, it would only be a propagandic, documentary text. It becomes literary

---

9 I talk about emigrants here in a fairly standard way. It should be noted, however, that an emigrant is not, at least generally speaking, a (political) refugee (see, e.g., EOHS 187). The emigrant community described in the work consists of two types of people. Those who left before the 1968 occupation are "emigrants" *simpliciter*, whereas "post-invasion" emigrants are "exiles."

precisely because of its ironic attitude—that is, as a result of the polyphony it contains. The function of absurdity and the absurd, however, is to question the credibility of the text. It plays against the veracity of the text and in doing so emphasizes the ontological autonomy of the work.

In *The Engineer of Human Souls*, the absurd is largely reserved for the social-ist world. Particular attention is given to the Czech secret police, whose activi-ties Smiricky experiences as a curious "art for art's sake," lacking any rational purpose:

But it's all too Dada. I remember suddenly an eighth pensioner who came to visit me with a message. His was a new variation: a message from my father. When I told the pensioner—all the while feeling embarrassed for him—that the only way he could have visited my father was with a candle on All Soul's Day, he was so alarmed that he almost knocked over his whiskey. He turned red and began sputtering a new version.

The message was, instead, from Smiricky's mother, the pensioner explains. In his satirical manner, Smiricky notes that this too was impossible, since his mother had "unfortunately" (from the point of view of the pensioner's tale) died before the father.

In connection with this rather outlandish account, Smiricky asks: "Are such enormous confusions really possible?" (EOHS 58). This overtness and bra-zenness of the secret police, even when facing detection, is a theme that the work takes up repeatedly. When a famous Czechoslovak poet arrives for a visit to Canada, a secret agent named "Ramses" poses as his interpreter:

"I mean," said Ramses, "I translate vot he say, zen vot you say. He talk, you talk, I translate."
"What he's trying to say," said Vokurovski, with barely a trace of an accent, "is that he's my interpreter."
"Zat's right," said Ramses. (EOHS 428)

Through such Kafkaesque incidents, Smiricky thus shows up the irrationality of the totalitarian regime, while at the same time defending common sense and obviously relishing in the victories he achieves through clear thinking. In this way—and in light of the arguments that I have presented already—the work can be read as highlighting the problematic nature of its central theme.

It defends reason by presenting these kinds of absurd situations, but at the same time it questions the effectiveness of rational explanations through a critique of logocentrism.

Even though Smiricky's focus is on critiquing totalitarianism, he does sometimes shift to questioning the Canadian situation too. This can be seen especially in minor matters; for example, in relation to the North American interpretation of the concept of freedom. Here, Smiricky recounts how a faculty colleague experiences it as a human rights violation to have been given an office without a window (EOHS 18–19). Doubts about the West take on a more serious tone when presented by an *alter ego* of sorts, Smiricky's Marxist student Hakim. Hakim claims, for instance, that Hawthorne was referring to America when he wrote: "Of all the varieties of mock-life, we have surely blundered into the very emptiest mockery, in our effort to establish the one true system" (EOHS 79). While Smiricky admits the possibility of such a reading, he nonetheless continues to emphasize that the ideal of a single "true" system belongs first and foremost to communism.

The work's few comments about the absurdities of North-American life are enough, however, to provide the necessary ironic counter-point, thus preventing the text from becoming overly ideological. These absurd features point to the similarity of the opposing political systems when (un)reason and (ir)rationality is taken to either extreme.

The overall ironic take of the work is clearest in an examination of its structural hints and codings and the subsequent break with the expectations these inspire. Pohorsky—an emigrant who has personally taken on the task of liberating Czechoslovakia and is referred to by Smiricky as "the savior of the nation" (EOHS 244)—provides a contemporary (in terms of the narrative present of the novel in 1970s Canada) structural representative, one might even say double, of the idealism that affected the young Smiricky's dissident dreams. Pohorsky's wild plans show a strong affinity with the young Smiricky's attempts to sabotage war efforts by producing defective machine-gun attachments for aircrafts.

Although Pohorsky's plans for the liberation of Czechoslovakia are presented as ridiculous in the narrative, their absurdity also quite deliberately foregrounds the absurd features of the communist regime (see EOHS 38, 192–193, 244–247, 477–478, and 539). Pohorsky's ideas include bringing down the Soviet five-year plan by calling on all Czechs to buy extra matches (EOHS 192–193) as well as causing nervous breakdowns to communist leaders and increasing the workload of the secret police beyond their capacity to handle. According to precise calculations, this latter objective could be realized by each emigrant simply sending a cryptic postcard to several leading Communists (EOHS 477–478).

Tellingly, Pohorsky dies in an explosion that he causes when trying to make letter bombs (EOHS 539). This proves that a Czech cannot act rationally since—as Smiricky notes—idiocy and stupidity are part or their national heritage (EOHS 238). The same Švejkianism (of which Pohorsky is clearly guilty) also flourishes in the wartime resistance: At the factory where the young Smiricky is forced to labour during the war, an old Czech named Nejezchleba proudly explains that he has avoided productive work by rolling the same three different-looking barrels from place to place for several years (EOHS 253).

Reason opposing the heart
An important dimension to the opposition of logocentrism in the work is in the reading that it offers of Joseph Conrad's *Heart of Darkness* and the related references to Prague as the dark place in the heart of Europe. (The novel speaks, for example, of "the pleasant Bohemian countryside preoccupied by darkness" [EOHS 48].) In Conrad's story, Charles Marlow is introduced to the senselessness of human actions on his journey to the heart of Africa; importantly, the irrationality and absurdity of things becomes more and more pronounced the further away he travels from European civilization. In *The Engineer of Human Souls*, Smiricky interprets Conrad's novel in a fairly typical way as a prophecy of a future totalitarian state and a saviour-figure like Kurtz. According to Smiricky, this prophecy came true with Stalin, whose actions released his country from rational behaviour (EOHS 368–369, 375–377, 462–464 and 480–482). Here, Smiricky links historical events closely with a broader history of ideas. This is particularly evident when he claims that the horror found in *Heart of Darkness* is the same as

... the horror of Marx's discovery, fully accepted by Lenin and made fully concrete by the will of the Generalissimo: that the only road to the future leads through a gateway made of the same material as Kurtz's fence. (EOHS 463)

The historical teleology suggested by Marx and Hegel has often been criticized for its dismissive attitude towards the suffering of individuals. Isaiah Berlin (1955, 23) goes so far as to say that their writings suggest a hint of malicious pleasure, "of sardonic gloating ... as they contemplate the discomfiture and destruction of the philistines, the ordinary men and women caught in one of the decisive moments of history." In that context, Smiricky's reading of *Heart of Darkness* is yet another critical comment on the idea of historical determinism and the underlying logocentrism.

Even the questioning of the "centre" is raised when Smiricky compares Czechoslovakia and the fear residing there to Conrad's Africa, to "fear from a heart of darkness, not from the Congo, but from a small one-time kingdom in the geographical centre of Europe, that continental appendage to the great land mass of Asia" (EOHS 99). Irony is once again dominant in the presentation: fear is in the heart of Europe, at its centre, but this centre is in fact on the fringes once a broader view of the world is assumed.

Although the *heart* is not explicitly in a symbolic role in *The Engineer of Human Souls*, setting it against reason seems justified. In this regard, it is interesting to note the ambivalent attitude of the work towards ideologies based on reason and a belief in some "centre": an overemphasis on rationality and reason is suspect, yet it is the heart that represents the darker side of human actions when listening to it might lead to absurdities. The compromise sought by the work offers the only credible alternative. Of course, the novel's title clearly signals this same conflict so often advanced between the soul and reason—the classic clash between free will and determinism—the latter represented here by social engineering based on mechanistic explanations.

Complex freedoms

In speaking of H. P. Lovecraft's classic novella *At the Mountains of Madness*, Smiricky compares the loathing and horror it expresses with Edgar Allan Poe's take on that same continent, wondering how Poe could—despite his own poverty and miserable conditions—also have dreamt of the freedom of the Antarctic: "the beautiful and ghastly freedom of the purple mountains of madness?... A pilgrimage of the soul? A pilgrimage *in* the soul" (EOHS 10). By comparing his own captivity in the German protectorate of Bohemia and Moravia with Poe's miseries, he also reveals the importance of his discovery of a similar internal landscape. This parallel to Poe's life is further emphasized through a number of references to Poe's tale *Ligeia*.[10]

The theme of captivity is important for the question of rationality too. Exis-

---

10 The thematic parallels between Poe's own life and his *Ligeia* are obvious: most notably the death of a young wife and drug addiction (although in Poe's case mistakenly attributed, it seems). *Ligeia* is even more interesting here, however, for introducing the idea of an invidual's capacity to beat death. This is a crucial refusal with respect to reason and logocentrism.

tentialist tones emerge powerfully in Smiricky's comments: "I was trapped once more in a cage, this time in a cage called Kolin. I seemed to carry my cage around with me" (EOHS 188). Even though detention and release is largely bracketed with respect to events in the novel—as already noted in connection with the silence concerning the flight from Czechoslovakia—it remains central to a structural reading.

The Engineer of Human Souls is divided into six chapters, named after the writers Poe, Hawthorne, Twain, Crane, Fitzgerald, Conrad and Lovecraft—all, conspicuously, authors who focus on describing the darker sides of human emotions. The first chapter begins by referencing Poe's description of the journey to the Southern Ocean (from The Narrative of Arthur Gordon Pym of Nantucket), indicating the centrality of the theme of captivity. The work also ends on a return to Antarctica through Lovecraft. Even though the isolation and silence of the Antarctic raises the theme of freedom, its significance is less straightforward when tied to these texts that focus on the horrors of the experience. However, reading these references only as expressions of a fear of freedom—following the ironic approach of the work—is called into question by a further intertextual reference: In speaking of the journey to Lovecraft's mountains of madness, to freedom, Smiricky says: "I've already been there" (EOHS 554)—an unmistakeable allusion, of course, to the final words of Twain's Huckleberry Finn ("I been there before"), which Smiricky also uses to dismiss Marxism (EOHS 140). In this way, the totalitarian regime is once again shown to parallel libertarian freedom.

In the same ironic vein, Smiricky highlights how the opposing systems drew closer to each other at the end of the 1970s, when the Czechoslovakian terror had reached new dimensions: a Czech cellist visiting Canada complains of how the communists had prevented the purchase of a Rococo-style hunting villa (EOHS 407).

The attitude towards the conflict between freedom and captivity—as well as towards that between the intellect and the emotions—is complex in The Engineer of Human Souls. The outcome is much the same as that in the theoretical conflict between the material and artistic aspects of a literary text; to such an extent, what is more, that the novel can be read as a comment on this textual problematic too. Both limitation and freedom are essential and unavoidable parts in any description or explanation; favouring one at the expense of the other only leads to aporia. At one extreme there awaits "horror;" at the other not only boredom or indifference but also the absurd, senseless actions these sentiments can inspire.

I would like to conclude this section by noting that, for Adorno art was, famously, a relatively autonomous part of culture—as a relatively independent discourse, one might say today (see, e.g., Van Den Braembussche 1990, 97; Bernstein 1992, 190–197). According to some of his interpreters, Adorno solves the problems of the autonomy of art, on the one hand, and of its intimate ties to broader society, on the other, by suggesting that the form of a work is what gives it a transhistorical dimension, with the content being only the material used for building that form.[11] Antoon Van Den Braembussche (1990, 98) goes further to say that social conflicts are always repeated in the structure of a work: "the unresolved antagonisms of social reality always reappear as the immanent problems of its form." According to this view, the "task" of art is to mediate in the resolution of conflicts within social reality. The suggestion seems to be, then, that a work of art receives its power from social conflict, and that in renewing the overall discourse of art, it also strives to offer opportunities for conflict resolution. The more important insight, however, is that although art is born in (and to an extent from) a specific social situation, it also has the freedom to create something that can transcend that situation.[12]

On Reading Historically

My primary goal here has been to show the significance as well as some of the limits of the autonomy of a literary text for its interpretation. If the text is read as an independent, worklike text, the conclusions and emphases of the reading are quite different to those reached when historical facts are sought at the expense of its other, internal and (inter)textual dimensions. Of course, historical inquiry should not aim at ignoring the historical context of a text. This kind of goal would be an impossible extreme for history. However, emphasizing context and historicity at such points that do not directly relate to the study of a work is equally extreme. Balancing between these

---

11 See, e.g., Van Den Braembussche (1990, 98). This is Van Den Braembussche's interpretation. Personally, I would not accept such a broad generalization in all situations but would also direct attention to how form follows material demands. For a crude example, think of how production realities constitute one directing factor for modernist design: the object has to be suited for mass-production. On the other hand, this simply means that art too is produced within the boundaries of realistic possibilities—how else? To me, Van Den Braembussche's idea is sufficient here as an introduction to the possibilities for invention, however.

12 An equally plausible but opposing argument can be found in *The Engineer of Human Souls*: "Form is almost always, to a greater or lesser extent, borrowed... What gives that form the taste of newness is content. Of course the basis of that content is the individual *uniqueness* of man, who lives out what *everyone* lives out: his unique variation on a general theme" (EOHS 391–392).

approaches is a problem that needs to be solved in any practical search for literary knowledge—always only on a case-by-case basis.

By connecting a literary text to broader ethical and philosophical problems, it can be read "historically" without submitting its worklikeness to unwarranted demands of truthfulness. This does not require that the significance of a text be evaluated in terms of its capacity to document events or particular historical conditions, for example. Nor does it mean that we attempt to discover in it the author's ideological valuations or compare it to other intellectual history sources *in terms of its reliability as a document.*

Instead, the significance of the kind of analysis that I have presented is in the way it allows us to consider the ideas that were possible in a given writing situation. This is not a matter of the truthfulness of a text, but rather involves the opportunities that it expresses. In the case of *The Engineer of Human Souls* as addressed here, attention was on the issue of Western rationality, on the value of logocentric thought. The work clearly shows that this question has been a poseable and relevant one already at the time of its writing. It is also obviously aware of the key problems of its time and tackles them in its meaning-making processes.

Each individual text functions, then, on the basis of the realities of its historical situation. Each literary text also works within the framework set by broader literary discourse (for the simple reason that if it did not, there would be no justification for calling it literature). Yet the existence, or at least development, of the discourse itself requires that each remark made in it somehow relate to the whole. Further, renewal might be postulated as a requirement for a particular text's being termed literary—for its inclusion in the literary canon. As textualist theories tend to suggest, each text is in some way a comment on earlier ones; yet, to be worklike, a text has to also offer something that departs from the tradition.

So—if the contents and ideas in a text are context-dependent, are they then also limited to that context? I have repeatedly here defended the claim that literary, worklike texts have two dimensions. Swingewood (1986, 34), from whom I presented a far more specific idea at the beginning of this text, nicely encapsulates this by saying that the work of art should be seen both as a poetic and as a historical phenomenon: "as both poetic and historical structure, an autonomous aesthetic form saturated with social meanings and human values that ultimately derive from everyday life... The meaning of an art-work is social and historical; it is also aesthetic." In this understanding, the "new" in the literary work might be argued to represent the aesthetic dimension. Does this mean that the only change fiction can bring about would relate to the literary tradition, or can literature impact society more broadly? That is, of course, a rhetorical question.

In crystallizing its context into a single image, as it were, in its formal coherence, a work captures and reiterates the social (power) relations, traditions and limiting structures of its time. It should be remembered though, that such structures can be studied only in specific phenomena: *structures exist only in their manifestations.* In interpreting such a manifestation, say a work of art, we cannot (as Pierre Bourdieu also reminds) expect it to be representative of a species or form or interpretable only through its own internal rules. The study of a work of art needs to take into account that the work is an expression of its time, and hence tied to the sociohistorical context of its genesis. *But* it also needs to be seen as *a work*, the impact of which does not stem from free-floating concepts or ideas (see Bourdieu 1989, 2). It is this independence from conceptual structures and interpretive apparatuses that offers the opportunity for a work to create those alternative "ideas" that do not already belong to the vocabulary of an era. This being the case, it would mean that aesthetic and intuitive actions can give rise to opportunities and horizons that could go beyond the ideological limits of a particular time. They might, in other words, be taken to increase—to paraphrase Lucien Febvre—the tools for thought that a particular era has at its disposal.

References

Bakhtin, Mikhail. 1991. *Dostojevskin poetiikan ongelmia.* Translated by Paula Nieminen and Tapani Laine. Helsinki: Kustannus Oy Orient Express.

Berlin, Isaiah. 1955. *Historical Inevitability.* London–New York–Toronto: Geoffrey Cumberlege, Oxford University Press.

Bernstein, J. M. 1992. *The Fate of Art: Aesthetic Alienation from Kant to Derrida and Adorno.* Cambridge and Oxford: Polity Press.

Blake, William. 1976 [written circa 1808]. *Annotations to Sir Joshua Reynolds's Discourses. Blake. Complete Writings.* Edited by Geoffrey Keynes. Oxford: Oxford University Press.

Bourdieu, Pierre. 1989. *Outline of a Theory of Practice.* Translated by Richard Nice. Cambridge: Cambridge University Press.

Derrida, Jacques. 1976. *Of Grammatology*. Translated by Gayatri Chakravorty Spivak. Baltimore and London: Johns Hopkins University Press.

Jay, Martin. 2013. "Intention and Irony: The Missed Encounter between Hayden White and Quentin Skinner." *History and Theory* 52(1): 32–48.

LaCapra, Dominick. 1987. *History, Politics, and the Novel*. Ithaca and London: Cornell University Press.

Nurmi, Martin K. 1975. *William Blake*. London: Hutchinson University Library.

Ricoeur, Paul. 1984. *Time and Narrative. Volume I*. Translated by Kathleen McLaughlin and David Pellauer. Chicago: University of Chicago Press.

Ronen, Ruth. 1994. *Possible Worlds in Literary Theory*. Cambridge: Cambridge University Press.

Škvorecký, Josef. 1984. *The Engineer of Human Souls: An Entertainment on the Old Themes of Life, Women, Fate, Dreams, the Working Class, Secret Agents, Love and Death*. Translated by Paul Wilson. London: Vintage.

Steiner, George. 1959. *Tolstoy or Dostoevsky*. Harmondsworth, Middlesex: Penguin Books.

Stern, J. P. 1992. *The Heart of Europe: Essays on Literature and Ideology*. Oxford and Cambridge, MA: Blackwell.

Swingewood, Alan. 1986. *Sociological Poetics and Aesthetic Theory*. London: MacMillan.

Van Den Braembussche, Antoon. 1990. "Rethinking Esthetics: Some Aspects of a General Science of Culture." In *Different Elements for a General Science of Culture*, 85–102. Aldershot, UK and Brookfield, USA: Avebury.

White, Hayden. 1987. *The Content of the Form: Narrative Discourse and Historical Representation*. Baltimore and London: Johns Hopkins University Press.

White, Hayden. 1994. "Foreword: Rancière's Revisionism." Foreword to *The Names of History: On the Poetics of Knowledge*, by Jacques Rancière, vii–xxi. Minneapolis: University of Minnesota Press.

NAMES

My race began as the sea began,
with no nouns, and with no horizon,
with pebbles under my tongue,
with a different fix on the stars.
But now my race is here,
in the sad oil of Levantine eyes,
in the flags of Indian fields.
I began with no memory,
I began with no future,
but I looked for that moment
when the mind was halved by a horizon.
I have never found that moment
when the mind was halved by a hori-
zon--
for the goldsmith from Bentares,
the stone-cutter from Canton,
as a fishline sinks, the horizon
sinks in the memory.
Have we melted into a mirror,
leaving our souls behind?
The goldsmith from Benares,
the stonecutter from Canton,
the bronzesmith from Benin.

A sea-eagle screams from the rock,
and my race began like the osprey
with that cry,

that terrible vowel,
that I!
. . . this stick
to trace our names on the sand
which the sea erased again, to our
indifference.

And when they named these bays bays,
was it nostalgia or irony? . . .

Where were the courts of Castile?
Versailles' colonnades
supplanted by cabbage palms
with Corinthian crests,
belittling diminutives,
then, little Versailles
meant plans for the pigsty,
names for the sour apples
and green grapes
of their exile. . . .

Being men, they could not live
except they first presumed
the right of everything to be a noun
The African acquiesced,
repeated, and changed them.

Derek Walcott

Can there be a Postmodern Nationalism?

*Kristin Rodier**

Abstract

In this paper I consider whether postmodern critique of the modern nation can furnish a normative theory about what to do in light of pre-existing national ties. I use Benedict Anderson's concept of imagined communities as a measure of shared identity and I engage with Zygmunt Bauman's critique of modernity and the adiaphorization of values. I answer Anthony Smith's objections to the postmodern critique of the nation and conclude by extrapolating a postmodern approach to national ties.

Introduction

The postmodern critique of the modern nation is thoroughgoing. If Zygmunt Bauman and Homi Bhabha—the postmodernists discussed in this essay— are both right about nationalism as a tool of control to alienate people from their free choice, then we would be hard pressed to justify national ties, static national identities, or perhaps any action in the name of "nations." As a critique of nationalism, postmodernism offers reasons for scepticism about nations in themselves. I think we are legitimate in asking postmodernists, "what ought we to do now?" What do we do about the seemingly legitimate claims that national ties make on us? Affects of patriotism and religion seem to be constitutive features of selves living in nations that are not easily changeable, as affects tend to be. How can postmodernism be brought to the living reality of nations without dismantling them in theory at the outset? I propose that this is indeed possible. The postmodern values of questioning social structures, promoting "true" individuality, taking responsibility for our moral selves, and engaging in cultural praxis that aims to "de-slime" strangers introduces a preliminary theory of the nation and subsequent national identities. In order to do this, we must assume a conception of the nation that would be both plausible and attractive to postmodernist. For this I turn to Benedict Anderson. This paper is not a defense of postmodernism nor the postmodern nationalism that it attempts to construct. Rather, its goal is to attempt to fold

* Kristin Rodier is a doctoral candidate of philosophy at the University of Alberta.

the postmodern critique into a concept of a nation that would be both recognizable and useful.

In order to sketch a notion of the nation that accounts for postmodern hesitations, I begin by analyzing the conceptual ambivalence that postmodernists argue constitutively signifies national identities. I tie this to Benedict Anderson's view of the nation as a collective imagining to strengthen the postmodernist's case. In section two, I unearth the conceptual underpinnings of the postmodern critique to make the postmodern critique speak for itself. I focus on Zygmunt Bauman because his postmodernism produces thick normative concepts that extend beyond critique. I argue against the objection that postmodernism is apolitical. I show that Bauman's characterization of modernity outputs a theory of solidarity with strangers meant to counteract a climate of fear and privatization of values. I also sift through modernity's effects on individuality and thus the ethical obligations that individuality implies. Bauman argues that our moral universe has shrunk in response to capitalism's pressure to perform; he asks that we revisit our ethical potential. Postmodern nationalism presents a tension between new paradigms of humanity that focus on "living liquid in a modern world." I thus turn to Anderson's work on language as a model for nationality that could be amenable to the postmodern critique of the nation. In the following three subsections, I look at the postmodern critique of modernity, the resultant ethics, and new paradigms of humanity that postmodernists bring to the problem of nationalism. I conclude that while Bauman in particular produces interesting concepts for thinking about the nation, his views need further expansion to account for nations and national identities.

I. "Qu'est ce qu'une nation?"

Perhaps we cannot exactly answer Ernest Renan's question in this paper, but it is important to interrogate what we mean by a nation.[1] National boarders are porous, and the internet and cheap modes of travel have added new transnational dimensions to everyday experience as daily contact can be made with people across national boundaries. It seems apt, then, to understand the nation as Anderson does, as an imagined community. As Anderson describes it, "an imagined community [is] both inherently limited and sovereign" (Anderson 1983, 6). One can imagine herself as part of a group, but

1 The title refers to Ernest Renan's (1832–92) influential lecture at the Sorbonne in 1882 where he posits a "civic" nationalism as opposed to an ethnic nationalism. His meditation on what constitutes a nation has been highly influential in French and other occidental nations.

only to a certain point; the group imagined is thought to possess autonomy to make independent decisions. I think this feature of imaging oneself as part of a community provides the bridge between Anderson and postmodernism.

Anderson's explanation of how imagining a community became possible is historical. First, modelled after how religions gained a monopoly of access to sacred languages, a specific conception and access to the ontological "truth" of a people was managed by governmental bodies entrusted with the author-ity to engender the ontological "truth" of a nation performatively through various institutional powers. Second, a concomitant belief held by the mem-bers of the community emerges that assigns the ability to define a nation as outside of one's self—that the truth of their nation comes from without. Lastly, with the advancement of novels and newspapers a certain conception of time led people to imagine the lives of others as steady, anonymous, and simultaneous (Anderson 1983, 14, 22, 26, 36). Anderson's historical account is perhaps dated in that centralized national definitional power oriented to reveal the "truth" of its people is now increasingly complex, but his technique remains pertinent—we ought to look to media, social media, politicians, pub-lic relations, and the structures of local and international governments to produce the complicated sites of authority that define Western nationhood.

Despite these complexities, participation in national activities rarely involves questioning the authorities that dispense the ontology of a nation's truth. Moreover, while participatory democracy is encouraged, there is a sense that one's nation is "above" one's personal definition of what it means to be of one's particular nationality. Much has changed since the invention of the printing press. However, the idea that who we imagine ourselves to be is governed by the techniques of media that allow us to think through the lives of others and how those lives are connected to ours constitute commu-nal experience. Imaginaries and narratives defining nationhood are unsta-ble, dense, and contestable. Nonetheless, citizens make sense of themselves in negotiation with a notion of citizenship deployed normatively to produce the ontological and moral "truth" of a nation. Contestation of the nation is, according to Homi Bhabha, guaranteed by the conceptual ambivalence of nationhood.

The internet and other forms of digital communication create possibilities for thinking of the nation as ambivalent. There are new awarenesses of how lives are lived in other places and this makes the project of self-imagining a tricky enterprise. In response, more is needed to define ourselves and secure recognition in this state of deep conceptual instability. Bhabha asks, "if the

ambivalent figure of the nation is a problem of its transitional history, its conceptual indeterminacy, its wavering between vocabularies, then what effect
does this have on the narratives and discourses that signify a sense of 'nation-
ness'?" (1990, 2). Anderson, according to Bhabha, fails to "read the profound
ambivalence" inherent in the idea of the nation. The ambivalence in national
narrations that is important for this paper is the splitting of the subject who
both narrates themselves as well as functions as the object of other narrations
(Bhabha 1990, 301, 311).

Bhabha underlines the ambivalent experience of living within a nation. He
writes that "the narrative of national cohesion can no longer be signified,
in Anderson's words, as a 'sociological solidity' fixed in a 'succession of plu-
rals'—hospitals, prisons, remote villages—where the social space is clearly
bounded by such repeated objects that represent a naturalistic, national horizon" (Bhabha 1990, 304-5). Furthermore, the nation is generally ambivalent;
persons are both subject to national orthodoxy, and as well as constitute that
orthodoxy. Even as, for example, the Occupy Wall Street movement occupies
Wall Street, it affirms the existence and so recognizes the profound importance of the institutions it desires to dismantle. The nation is also ambivalent in its temporality: "there is a split between the continuist, accumulative
temporality of the pedagogical and the repetitious, recursive strategy of the
performative," Bhabha states this is the difficulty in theorizing the time of the
nation—is it a present re-citation of its past self in discontinuous moments, or
is the nation an accumulation of its past events that necessarily strike out to
bring a determined future into existence (manifest destiny) (Bauman 1990,
297)? The nation is ambivalent in its narratives; nations contain both narratives and counter-narratives that "continually evoke and erase [the nation's]
totalizing boundaries" (Bhabha 1990, 300). The subject herself is not ambivalent but split nonetheless: even if subjects are able to narrate themselves
in some areas of their lives they still remain the objects of other narrations.
These ambivalences need careful attention when theorizing the nation and
nationalist narratives.

The postmodern critique of the nation as an ambivalent signifier works
with a conception of the nation as an imagined community. Anderson's view
is of a piece with postmodernism because treating the nation as an imagined
thing—or collection of narrations—supports postmodernism's main themes
of textuality, excess, uncertainty, and ambivalence. Bhabha writes that "the
address to nation as narration stresses the insistence of political power and
cultural authority in what Derrida describes as the 'irreducible excess of the

syntactic over the semantic'" (Bhabha 1983, 301). This is the idea that the formal properties of language have no choice but to signify that the semantic leaves a void or gap between the underlying syntax and surface semantics. This gap or void ends up signifying a semantic "quasi-void" (Gashé 1989, 13). Applying this Derridian idea to the nation, then, we see that the nation can be an imagining or set of imaginings, a narrative or set of narratives that share the feature of undecidablility. There is no one and only narrative or imagining that will define, say, "Germanness" or "Canadianness," but there will be a collection of national narratives told about each noun that tries to signify itself. Citizens, too, are left to make meaning out of these areas of quasi-void and semantic excess, thereby adding semantic agency to citizens who narrate themselves into a national project.

An important place of agreement between Anderson and the postmodernist is the idea that the nation does not tap a deep-seated or ontological desire for a national identity (*pace* primordialism), nor does it provide an outlet for otherwise frustrated (and perhaps sublimated) naturally existing emotional ties to nation, country, or society writ large informed by the historical continuity nations have through time (*pace* perennialism). The nation is a construct belonging to the territory of, at least, the imagination. According to the postmodern critique, the particular content of the imagining is, however, not as straightforward as Anderson writes. How can the ambivalence of the nation identified by the postmodernists be amenable to a theory of the nation?

II. Asking the Postmodern Critique to "Speak for Itself"

In the following three sub-sections, I ask the postmodern critique to "speak for itself." This means laying bare both the background assumptions informing the critique of modernity that make the postmodern "post" and its implicit prescriptive dimensions that map a preliminary picture of a postmodern nation. An immediate objection to this strategy would be that *prime facie* a postmodern nation is either paradoxical or contradictory. For example, Anthony D. Smith argues against the postmodern critique by saying that it undermines the basic assumptions of modernism so fervently that it must disbelieve in the "sociological reality of nations, and the power of nationalist ideologies" (Smith 1998, 202). Turning the postmodernist into a caricature of Cartesian scepticism about nations is not a charge that a postmodernist should have to answer. However, if we try to tease apart the tension between the postmodern framework and a modern view of nations, we may find an

objection worth countering. I see two objections to a postmodern nationalism; one in general, and one in particular. In general, it is impertinent to
ask a critique to also have an implicit constructive view about future actions
and responses to the nation. In particular, the postmodern agenda is only
concerned with testing the limits and de-centering concepts that were once
taken for granted, and in principle, it does not aim to replace these categories. My modest goal is to show that these objections are merely tensions and
not devastating criticisms. In this section, I would like to argue that the postmodern critique implies a backdrop of assumptions that create an analyti-
cally usable idea of the nation and national identities. I make this argument
on two grounds: first, just because the nation is ambivalent and uncertain
does not mean that it is non-existent or of no moral or political import (if at
least because Derrida writes that at least at first it is a condition of possibility
for thinking concepts that we theorize "as if" the conceptual indeterminacy
is not fatal to our theorizing), and second, the postmodernist's backdrop of
critique implies central concepts that can be both illuminated and useful in
constructing a view about nations, and in prescribing a response to current
nations and national identities, especially that of Zygmunt Bauman. I thus
mainly focus on his approach to postmodernism.

Bhabha writes, "if the problematic 'closure' of textuality questions the
'totalization' of national culture, then its positive value lies in displaying the
wide dissemination through which we construct the field of meanings and
symbols associated with national life" (Bhabha 1990, 5). Here, "national life"
is treated as an existing thing worthy of inquiry despite or perhaps because
of the kind of "closure" and "totalization" that is effected. By Bauman's lights,
a prescriptive dimension for the nation involves at least three positive values;
the right of each person to a "truer" individuality, embracement of the uncertainty "embodied" by society's "strangers," and in general the de-polarization
of conceptual space that has heretofore theorized the nation. Specific explanations of these concepts will take place in the remaining three sub-sections
of section II of this essay, but for now preliminary plausibility of the inquiry
is demonstrated by highlighting the prescriptive and conceptual importance
placed on theorizing the nation and national identities provided by the postmodern critique.

As Clare Hemmings (2011) argues, defining postmodernism (broadly
construed) in feminist theory as apolitical relies on a certain conception of
political temporality. Indeed, the "post" in "postmodern" itself gives us an
idea of the temporality of movements or politics that imbue the present with

a kind of theoretical teleology as though we are going beyond our wrong-headed past, figured in this case as an attachment to modernism. Hemmings argues that feminist theorists tell stories about their own past that rob it of its complex history. For example, "decade-fixing" is a way of partitioning certain views into blocks of time and as time passes, the ideas become out of date in the rush to remain current (Hemmings 2011, 48).[2] Feminist flirtations with postmodernism have resulted in the charge of being apolitical, getting too involved in the academy, in abstractions, and in general losing connection to the everyday experiences of women. Hemmings identifies this as a "loss" narrative, as in "we have lost the good old days of doing real politics." These narratives construct an affect of loss against the postmodernist. Hemmings (2011, 83) writes:

> Subjects of progress and loss narratives insist on their absolute separation from one another, missing the ways in which they utilize and instantiate a common historiography, missing the ways in which that historiography grounds post-, quasi-, or antifeminist claims as well.

Postmodernism as the name for a cluster of theorists cannot be implicated in this temporality of progress. Indeed, postmodern theory is attempting to disrupt theories of linear time, including that of progress beyond modernism. The supposed temporal fixing in the name of "postmodernism" can lead to straw person analyses like that of Smith's "Beyond Modernism?" in which it is presumed that the postmodernist is failing her own project should she not be fully "beyond" any trace of nations or modernism. It is no wonder that he charges postmodernists with having no sense of history (Smith 1998, 199, 218).

In a last thrust against this charge, I offer Allan Hutchinson's response to

---

2 A prime example of the history-erasing effects of "decade fixing" can be found in Anthony Smith; "Early feminist analyses did not seek to address the issues of ethnicity and nationalism, but from the mid-1980's there has been a growing literature in this area" (Smith 1998, 205). These claims are patently false (Harriet Taylor Mill, Mary Wolstencraft, Emma Goldman, Charlotte Perkins Gilman, Simone de Beauvoir just to name the glaring erasures) and erase a history of cross-racial collaboration and involvement between anti-racist and feminist struggles. This also leads to a disavowal of other feminist work that predates the 1980's as racist and decontextualized, and not properly political (Audre Lorde, Mary Daly, Shumalith Firestone, Betty Friedan, Angela Davis, and Germaine Greer, just to name the glaring counterexamples). Smith's gloss on feminist history buys into a progress narrative where with new information, feminist theorizing has come to better understand issues of "ethnicity and nationalism" in the present than they did in the past. This teleology of theory belies the complicated interconnectedness of different ideas that came to be in feminist history and effects an erasure of the internal tensions and disagreements that make feminist theory such a productive site of critique.

the terse but succinct: "Can postmodernism deliver the political goods?" In struggling against the objection that the overly theoretical character of post-modernism breeds political quietism and acquiescence, he writes:

> While postmodernism rejects the metaphysical privileging of grand theory, it most certainly does not deny the worth of social, historical or political theorizing. Provided that it is suitably provisional, revisable, and contextual, such theorizing is at the heart of a transformative political praxis. In rejecting History, it does not ignore the lessons of history, and in rejecting Telos, it does not eschew the value of criticism. As all claims are located within a dynamic set of social practices, postmodernism insists that all theorizing pay attention to the structural circumstances of that social milieu and, in particular, to theorizing its own embeddedness in such historical contexts. Critical insight is a prelude to transformative action. (Hutchinson 1992, 779)

In occupying conceptual space as a tool of critique, postmodernism is already in dialogue with conceptions of the nation, and can then imply a conceptual reformulation of the nation.

III. Modernity

If postmodern is not "post" or "beyond" modernity temporally, but rather is philosophically opposed to modernity, then what features of modernity are at issue? While Bhabha is the quintessential postmodern theorist of the nation, I look to Bauman on modernity because his critique is most fruitfully value-laden and postmodern, thus suited to construct a postmodern national-ism. Bauman locates the genesis of modernity in the human urge for "order-building." No particular order is thus ingrained as primordial or necessary; only *that* we want to build order is guaranteed. This denial of a necessary or determinate social structure that humanity aims at in order-building moti-vates Bauman's critique of modernity. Detractors would lament that these order-building projects are what bring progress. However, Bauman disagrees. He writes:

> It was the State that knew what order should look like, and which had enough strength and arrogance not only to proclaim all other states of affairs to be disorder and chaos, but also force them to live down to such a condition. This was, in other words, the modern state – one which leg-

islated order into existence and defined order as the clarity of binding divisions, classifications, allocations and boundaries. (Smith 1997, 18)

This goes against Anthony Smith's claim that postmodernists have no sense of how the modern nation was developed (Smith 1998, 219). Senses of how the modern nation was developed emerged due to a desire to make sense of the world by categorizing our experiences. Much like in Walcott's poem "to trace our names on the sand / which the sea erased again, to our indifference," we see that the logic of order building is that which wants to break up and partition the original or pre-linguistic states of nature. A direct line is drawn between order-building, colonization and the modern nation in Walcott's work.

Bauman argues that the effects of "order-building" are paradoxical in that they reveal the "permanent and irreducible" conditions of uncertainty that underlie the nation because no amount of order-building can guarantee personal security (Bauman 1997, 21). In legislating behaviour according to the logic and order of the modern nation, people have not flourished. Instead of increasing freedom, these "powers" have eroded human ties and made us "live down" to its categories of failure. Not only does order-building not create the safety that is its expressed purpose, but it creates the disorder that underwrites the feelings of uncertainty that come from uncontainable social realities.

As a reaction to the modern legislation of order, the current conditions of uncertainty are contingent on this particular historical moment of modernity. Here, certainty is signified by the identities that adhere to the logic of sense; the businessman, his beautiful wife and cisgender children. In considering context, the postmodernist criticizes modernity where it stands—as profoundly capitalist, deregulated, and individualistic (I would add neoliberal, postfeminist, and post-racial). Concentrating on this approach to modernity, Bauman argues that the free, natural, human desire to build order gets frustrated and transmutes into an atmosphere of ambient fear (Bauman 1997, 22).

Bauman explains the fear by pointing to many factors. Since the so-called "Second World" has disintegrated and the "Third World" is challenging "First World" conceptions of happiness and progress, the psychological effects of *laissez-faire* capitalism leads to fear of market guarantees for future jobs through market supremacy, rather than talent, skill or hard work.[3] Nevertheless, the ideology of the self-made man as a reaction formation against proletarian critique is alive and well. While running for the Republican presidential nomination in 2012, Herman Cain said in an interview, "if you do not have a job and you aren't rich, blame yourself."[4] In this post-Reagan neoliberal environment, the social safety nets that local relationships and collectivities previously provided waned in response to the availability of resources through the free-market because local others do not work together to meet the needs of the collective. Additionally, the rise of "episodic time" assures us that we are only a "channel change" away from a new self—memory, like video tapes, may be wiped clean—we can abruptly change identity as quickly as we can imagine new possibilities (Bauman 1997, 22–25). Or, with the rise of websites like ashleymadison.com, you are only one click away from being cheated on (tagline: "Life's short. Have an affair."). How can we trust when connections are episodic and marked by fear? Further, under the spectre of uncertainty, strangers are no longer clear, definable, and hence, "eradicable," but rather, they are here, with us and within us. Identity building, which used to be a gradual and steady process (read: as belonging to "repetitive societies" per Marx's analysis) is now "poorly founded...erratic and volatile" (Bauman 1997, 25). Indeed, if you have a solid, definable, and persistent identity in contemporary neoliberal capitalism it is a liability and not an asset (Bauman 1997, 27). Since there is no all-encompassing social structure or theory that can account for humanity there are gaps in which the order-building tendency of modernity excludes or suppresses any person or group that represents this fundamental flaw in their reasoning. The interstitial members of communities, in Bauman's words the "slimy strangers," symbolize the arbitrary and incomplete nature of modernity's order-building logic.

Certain people are strangers because they have a tendency "to befog and eclipse boundary lines which ought to be clearly seen" (Bauman 1997, 25).

---

3 It is definitely possible to challenge Bauman on this point. Brazil, Russia, India, and China (BRIC) are nearing if not already achieving Second-World status. Further to the point of market security, Meme Roth, an anti-obesity advocate has said in an interview with Bill O'Reilley, "If I'm China and I'm India, and I'm looking out economically at this country, I'd say, 'You know what? Keep your processed foods. You American, you get fatter, you get sicker, and we're on the way'" (*The O'Reilly Factory*, March 11, 2007).

4 http://www.nydailynews.com/news/politics/herman-cain-occupy-wall-street-protesters-rich-blame-article-1.961517

Bauman draws this concept from Sartrean existential psychoanalysis, wherein the stranger comes to symbolize powerlessness:

If I dive into the water, if I plunge into it, if I let myself sink into it, I experience no discomfort, for I do not have any fear whatsoever that I may dissolve in it; I remain a solid in its liquidity. If I sink in the slimy, I feel that I am going to be lost in it...to touch the slimy is to risk being dissolved in sliminess. (Sartre 1956, 777)

Encountering the slimy is coming to realize that we are not in ultimate control of who we are and what other people may be. The fact that I cannot swim inconsequentially through the slime shows me the great power of the slime: "[We] react in a wild, rabid, distraught and flustered fashion, as one reacts to the incapacitating pulling/dissolving power of the slimy. The sliminess of strangers, let us repeat, is the reflection of their own powerlessness. It is their own lack of power that crystallizes in their eyes as the awesome might of the strangers" (Bauman 1997, 29). How can a powerlessness be also an "awesome might?" A concrete example of this would be the "strange sliminess" of feminists that want to "corrupt" women's "natural" role as mothers and wives. Organizations like "Ladies Against Feminism" try to coax women back into traditional roles with an emphasis on the naturalness of these roles. But, if they did not believe that the "sliminess" of feminists would "stick to them" they wouldn't have to struggle so hard against this "deviant" force. Anti-feminist groups know or at least implicitly demonstrate that the alterity of the other constitutes a kind of threat; it highlights their own lack of freedom and hence the freedom of the other.

How should we respond to the "slimy" and the "strange?" One response will be a kind of humanism that will be further explored in the next section, but preliminarily we need to re-think "the human" that informs our humanism. Traditional humanism is too "fraternal" (overemphasizing sameness) and a postmodern humanism would focus on actively either "de-sliming" strangers or embracing strangeness and difference or some combination of both. As we shall see, this is not merely the liberal value of tolerance, but it goes further than that: Tolerance is acknowledging the strangeness within ourselves and in others (Tester 2004). Bauman advocates that ethics needs transformation from tolerance to solidarity: "whereas tolerance is a fate (since it is a reflection of the endemic ambivalence of postmodernity), solidarity is a destiny because it has to be chosen responsibly" (Bauman 1997, 148). The de-sliming of strangers is not just something I do for others, but it is part of my destiny also. According to Bauman we must join the fight for recognition of everyone's difference, not merely tolerating each other in quietism, thus changing the way we approach national ties (Bauman 1997, 147).

This characterization of modernity can be disputed: indeed, it is difficult to know if this captures every person's experience in even the most typical of "modern" nations. We might also ask after Bauman's characterization of groups and societies that are resisting this trend. However, in keeping with the project of this paper let us assume that this characterization is mostly right— that is, that the modern nation embodies uncertainty despite its attempts to hold onto logic, order, and nationalistic affect for compelling obedience from its citizens.[5] This characterization is necessary in order to set into motion the response that the postmodernist prescribes for us in our interactions with each other, and importantly, with nations and national identities. So far we have learned that the postmodern critique of modernity implies that, as a reaction to modernity we both try to respect that order-building cannot and should not be legislated on a mass scale, and that we ought to take on solidarity with the other in order to de-slime strangers.

IV. Individuality and Ethics

How do we understand ourselves within a nation? Especially with social media, the concept of the individual is changing and so is the nation. An important postmodern theme, or value, is individual choice, however, the concept of the individual and the ethics it makes possible needs to be folded into the postmodern nation being sketched here. How individuals relate ethically is a touchstone of national identities and must be considered by a postmodern nationalism.[6] Bauman gives the familiar criticism of modern individualism, namely that it is characterized by the "individualization" of persons as atomistic and solitary. This interpellation is effected within a dreaming collective.

---

5 It does not go unnoticed that the characterization of modernity may in fact be missing out on the post-colonial resistance inherent in, for example, Partha Chatterjee's response to totalizing descriptions of modernity. His point is that characterizing society in such broad structural strokes misses the "internal" dimension of persons' experiences, especially of the colonized; "nationalism declares the domain of the spiritual its sovereign territory and refuses to allow the colonial power to intervene in that domain...The colonial state, in other words, is kept out of the 'inner' domain of national culture" (Chatterjee 1997, 217).

6 In David Miller's *On Nationality* (1995) he argues that national identities are justified because they are a vehicle for ethical claims that can promote liberal tolerance, diversity, and human rights.

The only way to support individualization of this kind is with ideology, or fol-lowing Walter Benjamin, Bauman argues that:

> The collective was "dreaming" because "it was unconscious of itself, com-posed of atomized individuals, consumers who imagined their commod-ity-dreams to be uniquely personal (despite all objective evidence to the contrary), and who experienced their membership in the collectivity only in an isolated, alienating sense, as an anonymous component of the crowd." To put this in a nutshell – The collective was 'dreaming' because it made the individuals who composed it unaware of the collective origins of their individual qualities and experiences and of the collective nature of their troubles (Bauman 2000, 86).

Ironically, the more we channel our moral energy into self-protection and our own personal well-being, the more that our moral universe shrinks. An example of the privatization of values is the prevalence of gated communi-ties in modern capitalist society. Inversely, public society becomes a space of anonymity:

> This new medium of living is, like other media, a message—and the par-ticular message which this medium conveys is that 'values and morals' are for domestic use only and that the sole way to preserve them and practice is to separate, to disengage, to exclude and to withdraw. (Bau-man 2000, 84)

The effects of this ethical withdrawal takes many forms; we shy away from social/communal arrangements, dependency is transvaluated into a bad thing (we rebuke the "too clingy" or the "too touchy-feely"), and the subject, in her individualization, is separated from the social conditions that make choice possible. Bauman says that it is a misreading of modernity to argue that these vehicles of separation increase available choices. We are dreaming that freedom lies in a new and improved consumer product. The effect is rather that we have a more limited ability to question, resist, and shape the structures to which we are systematically subject (Bauman 2000, 89).

Bauman furthers his case by arguing that individualization is inversely pro-portionate to the retreat of God. Banished further than Romeo from Verona, is the soul from the conceptual landscape of contemporary sociology. The disappearance of "soul" stands for the retreat of ethicality and then so for indifference. By Bauman's lights "indifference" comes:

> In the wake of the decision to exclude certain areas of life, and above all the beings who populate such areas, from the set of legitimate reasons to be concerned and to take sides. 'Indifference' stands for an active rejection of engagement, for ethical un-concern. It is the attitude taken towards the objects, also (above all) such as happen to be human subjects, which have been first banished from the universe of moral obligation. (Bauman 2000, 92)

In short, the indifferent avoid responsibility and subsequently human bonds wilt and fade. A shrinking of the moral universe, an atrophy or attenuation of morality is achieved through what Bauman names a process of "adiaphorization." This process is covert and tacit, its effects seen in "staving off the very possibility of [a] certain category of others appearing as targets of ethically meaningful action" (Bauman 2000, 92). As the amount of action not amenable to moral judgment increases we find a desert landscape in its place: we are left to fashion new concepts, new behaviours, and new institutions that attempt to fill this void. Two stages follow: first the panoptic, bureaucratic order-building forces of modernity and then the more dubious power relations of seduction and precariousness (Bauman 2000, 93). It is the latter river in which we now swim. We become seduced by "managerial wisdom" that "washes its hands" of personal, ethical engagement with employees under the rubric of freeing people to tap the heretofore untapped resources of "human talents, initiative and ingenuity" (Bauman 2000, 94). Precariousness takes the shape of being a disposable worker or lover, working either a McJob (say, at Starbucks), or not being able to "handle a relationship right now."

What are the results of this shrinking of the moral universe? The Other and I become similarly situated in a universe where we owe little to each other: "Refusing responsibility for the Other is a wise and noble thing to do; and I should be grateful to all the others who reciprocate in the same manner" (Bauman 2000, 95). Human interactions are increasingly included in the amoral, external, non-reciprocal relationships (i.e., "I'm not here to make friends"). Donald Trump is famous for saying, "it's nothing personal, it's just business." This sentiment echoes closely Bauman's point that when you dissolve the collectivity (with added value that this will be good for you), you render possible networks of dependency and support seemingly inaccessible. The logical question to then ask this critique is what we do now. What does ethical action look like and how ought we to struggle against modernity's adiaphorization of our moral universe? We get a clue about this from Bauman's 1995 work *Life in Fragments: Postmodernity and Morality in which he draws a distinction between ethics and morality*. In modernity, ethics is externally imposed, universally founded, requirements of law that are likened to the biblical Moses' tablets of stone taken down from the mountain with inscribed unconditional commandments (Tester 2004, 141). These universals give people confidence in their lives and in the rightness of their choices. By contrast, postmodern morality does not guarantee this same certainty: A postmodern morality does not need "codes or rules, reason or knowledge, argument or conviction" (Tester 2004, 143) What should inform ethical action is both guiding and sustaining inter-human togetherness, which obtains in a context of irreducible ambivalence and uncertainty—a difficult and embodied experience of openness to the other and openness to the new and slimy. The laws that forcefully impose ethical duties are the "solids" of modernity that melt away our pre-existing ethical responsibility with the other will hopefully flourish and bind us together. The exciting reversal effected is that the laws that are supposed to command ethical relationship preclude them.

With this analysis, we can make sense of Bauman's claim that taking responsibility for the ethicality of our selves is the "birth-act" of morality. Contra the Kantian and neo-Kantian intuition (for example) of ethics that use principles of reason to constrain action in order to output ethicality, our beings are already permeated with ethicality. As a reference, we have thought it useful to write down these rules to externalize our knowledge and supposedly better regulate ethicality. However, this "rulebook" approach to ethics simply alienates us from our primordial ethical knowledge of our connectedness with others. Nonetheless, it is not enough to be made aware of our existential connection to the other. We must also move from the level of "being-with" to a "being-for", which will prove difficult in the face of the awesome might of strangers—the slimy other. He writes, "taking up responsibility for the Other is the birth-act of morality. It is not, though, a one-of [sic] event. The birth act is re-enacted repeatedly in the life of the moral self... Once born, its survival is never assured" (Bauman 2000, 82). Bauman's claim is that when we recognize our ontological responsibility our moral responsibility increases.

According to the postmodern critique, modernity over-individualizes, which causes ethical adiaphorization and emotional climate of suspicion and fear. The faith entrusted in the ethical norms of society has dwindled and the worry is that possibilities for a safe and secure life are foreclosed. This next section explores how to respond to the Other in light of these changes to ethics.

V. A New Paradigm of National Identities

Liquid life is a succession of new beginnings – yet precisely for that reason it is the swift and painless endings, without which new beginnings would be unthinkable, that tend to be its most challenging moments and most upsetting headaches. (Bauman 2007, 107)

How do we apply this exposition of modern ethics to a view of identities—and national identities in particular? A view of national identities needs to be responsive to a new paradigm of humanity. Bauman writes; "[We should focus] on the right to choose one's identity as the sole universality of the citizen/human, on the ultimate, inalienable individual responsibility for the choice ... The chance of human togetherness depends on the rights of the stranger, not on the question who—the state or the tribe—is entitled to decide who the strangers are" (Bauman 1997, 33). This focus on the rights of the stranger to be strange asks society to begin to define ourselves positively instead of negatively. A legacy of modernity (that at least, Jean-Paul Sartre would argue is necessary) is that we feel threatened and scared of the other—especially the strange or "slimy" other.[7] According to the postmodernist, however, we must work to embrace difference, ambivalence, and uncertainty in national identities. We are responsible for fighting in solidarity for the rights of each other to self-identify, rather than using statehood to define identity. If my neighbor chooses to identify with a resistance group near or far, I should I should be standing-with and being-for her choice. National identities are a paradigm example of things we may find slimy or strange because they

---

7 In his work, *Being and Nothingness*, Sartre argues that what takes place in confronting another consciousness is that you are made object for another subject. He writes: "Thus for the Other I have stripped myself of transcendence... This is accomplished, not by any distortion ... but by [the Other's] very being." Even if it is not necessarily conflictual, it seems apparent that being-made-object (stripped of transcendence) by the other is tied strongly to being ashamed of oneself. I mention this side-note to show that it appears plausible that there are limits to Bauman's prescription to de-slime the stranger (Sartre 1966, 353).

color our accents, comportments, desires, families, and traditions. Bauman suggests that we respond with solidarity and tolerance and resist legislation that favors modern "order-building" techniques. We should value difference among national identities and narratives—or at least those that also preserve inter-human togetherness by looking for what binds us together.

Some concepts for the postmodernist are determinate; we are charged with the task of creating and challenging social structures and also with the task of embracing strangeness in others and ourselves. Bauman is clear that leaving the individual to create her own culture from cultural praxis changes focus from structures to structuring. The nation, according to this view, is not a clear, definable mega-structure with determinate rules for national identities. Rather, the focus turns to taking a cultural stance in which one challenges and eclipses prefabricated (national) identities and boundaries (Marotta, 38–39).

VI. The Twisted Road to a Postmodern Nation

Is this a nationalism? Bauman worries that "one needs, after all, only to drive a few miles to refill the empty tank of nationalism with racist fuel" (Bauman 2007, 29). While Bauman is suspicious of nationalistic ties, Anderson emphasizes how national ties are akin to familial love (because they are not chosen) but are also an unconditional disinterested love (Bauman 2007, 144). This provides a qualitative difference between identities:

Dying for one's country, which usually one does not choose, assumes a moral grandeur which dying for the Labour Party, the American Medical Association, or perhaps even Amnesty International cannot rival, for these are all bodies one can join or leave at easy will. (Bauman 2007, 184)

Anderson draws a distinction between the gravity implied in a national identity and the affability involved in the choice of other kinds of identity. Why this grandeur? Why are national identities different than any other? Anderson believes that beyond qualities that were traditionally associated with a nation (race, religion, and so on) the common factor is language. Language is both primordial and able to be adopted by others. He writes; "For it shows that from the start the nation was conceived in language, not in blood, and that one could be 'invited into' the imagined community" (Anderson 1983, 144). Common language connects us both affectively with the dead and temporally with other speakers in a contemporaneous community. This begins to appear as a threshold for blending in the postmodern critique. Anderson continues, "seen as both a historical fatality and as a community imagined through language, the nation presents itself as simultaneously open and closed" (Anderson 1983, 146). Would the postmodernist accept the amount that identities are also "closed" in Anderson's terms? An imagined community is open because one can learn a language (albeit with her own accent) and become part of an imagined community. The community is also limited by capacity and time—one can only learn so many languages in a lifetime and it takes time to learn a language. This explanation of national identities puts limits on what imagined community one can claim to inhabit. Would postmodernists accept this criterion on imagined communities?

Smith argues against the postmodernist on this point. He accuses them of vying for "voluntary-ethnicity" which is not a proper option because people are restricted by ethnic history and political geography (Smith 1998, 205). Using the examples of "you can't just choose to be Chinese or Turkish," Smith has stacked the deck in his favor by only picking confirming examples. He says that voluntary ethnicity has not worked in the past, but that is but proof that the postmodern critique needs to further work to shift understandings of identities so that they can include room for voluntary adoption and less "slimy" strangers. Moreover, we do not need to read Bauman's claim as strongly supporting "voluntary ethnicity" because it can be a call for the recognition of the right of someone to identify herself within a nation in the way that she wants, not that she can create an identity by fiat. At the same time, Smith has stacked the deck in his favor by choosing particular examples that are least amenable to a voluntarist approach to identity, which turns his view of national identity into death-by-counter example. This is because, unlike the postmodernist, he is trying to find necessary and sufficient conditions for a national identity. If instead we looked at national identities as having a family resemblance with each other; some appear more voluntarist, some less so, some have overlapping ethnicities, some do not but they all constitute national identities that are recognized within the usage of the term, then we can better explain why some of his points work better with reference to what he terms "immigrant nations" like Canada and Australia (which should really be labelled colonial nations) and that do not work well with other national identities.[8]

---

8 Voluntary identification in Canada, for example, seems to have its own unique marriage-like character much like a hyphenated last name; one is French-Canadian, Irish-Canadian, Western-

If our sole right is to choose identity, then we appear to have a substantial tension between postmodernism and nationalism. Anderson has national identities as both closed and open, malleable and fixed. However, the post-modernist does not provide us with criterion for understanding affiliation with one identity over another. As a result, we might be forced to support eve-ryone's choices, so long as they do not promote a view of an other that turns them into slimy strangers. The concreteness of national identities is more akin to the primordialness yet adaptablility of our ability to have and adopt languages. Barring physical and physiological barriers, the postmodern ideal of allowing, promoting, and preserving difference, choice, and change may be made consonant with Anderson's view of national identities as closely tied to languages and unchosen factors in one's life. However, this would only be if postmodernists have overshot their own goal. In order to promote the val-ues they hold—questioning social structures, promoting local order-building, and solidarity—they need not have a notion of persons as free and malleable. Anderson's view might give the liquid self a container to hold what it can also allow to be fluid and free. This tension arises from both having an ideal of unlimited free choice and not blending in a concrete notion of how it would apply to our daily lives—a shortcoming of the postmodern view.

VI. Further Questions for the Postmodernist

"Does this constitute any kind of nationalism we would want?" is the real ques-tion. Would, for example, Canadians be willing to stop mulling the question of what it means to be Canadian and be satisfied with the language model offered in this paper (this is especially tricky given that Canada has two offi-cial languages)? The promise of new individuality that focuses on taking back the moral world from adiaphorization might be motivating for the members of a pre-existing nation to adopt a postmodern stance toward their nation, but I am skeptical of putting trust in the promise of inter-human togetherness grounded upon ontologically connected moral selves, especially since collec-tive imaginings are inherently limited and sovereign. This asks at least two separate questions; first, is this theory something that would function at the

---

Canadian, Métis-Canadian, and interestingly the shift away from Native Canadian to Indigenous or Aboriginal is a divorce from Canada, a new assertion of national identity under colonial rule. Canadian Broadcasting Corporation host Rex Murphy recently gaffed during a call-in show by asking someone if they were Muslim-Canadian or Canadian-Canadian. This redoubling shows the family resemblance quality of national identities and while Smith wants to call this fragmentation, understanding identities in terms of family resemblance can deal with the complexity of individual identities and yet the overlapping qualities that constitute national ties.

practical level? Is it attractive at the theoretical level? A cost-benefit analysis between accurate ontological foundations (the claim that real human connectedness is of this sort rather than that and we ought to promote this foundational claim) and immediate practical concerns (what to do with existing nations, national identities, and claims of exclusionary sovereignty?) needs to be done at another time.

How far can we push the dichotomy between the "logic of modernity" which strives for order-building at a large scale and the "local" order-building that Bauman advocates? Is there a significant "in-between" yet to be explored? The answers to these questions have consequences for the specifically nationalistic worry about state sovereignty and what kind of legislation the postmodernist would accept. The tension between local and macro order-building is again difficult to because for Anderson, imagined communities are inherently limited—we cannot imagine all people who simultaneously live under all narratives—and so will have to limit our imaginings. But what does this do for the seemingly global claims that the postmodernist makes? It is my suspicion that we are going to rely on something more foundational like language—as Anderson writes—and then it is clear that the postmodernist's critique of modernity as a constructive view of nations leaves us unsatisfied. Though the tensions between nationalism and postmodernism are not devastating, Bauman—the most normatively robust postmodernist—needs to explain what he wants of nations: what constitutes a stranger, how does one deslime the stranger, how is that different than liberal tolerance and how do we manage being ethically connected to each other when our imagined communities are inherently limited and sovereign? Though Bauman gives us the tools to understand the beginning of a postmodern nation, even coupling his view with Anderson's imagined communities still leaves us wonting for a robust view of nations amenable to lived experience of national identities.

There is no returning to that moment before language and, by extension, before national ties. To return to the opening poem of this essay, we live in a time after the sea-eagle cried out from the rock and gave a first division of our selves into an "I." In the same way as the colonial forces that brought their dividing nouns to the colonized, there is no going back to an unnamed bay, a name in the sand wiped away by the tide. What we can do now is repeat and change the existing languages that we have inherited, and to repeat and change our national ties so that they include the possibility of changing not only our national understandings but ourselves in our encounters with others.

References

Anderson, Benedict. 1983. *Imagined Communities*. New York: Verso.

Bauman, Zygmunt. 2007. *The Contemporary Bauman*. New York: Routledge.

———. 2000. "The Ethics of Individuals." *Canadian Journal of Sociology / Cahiers canadiens de sociologie* 25(1): 83–96.

———. 1997. *Postmodernity and Its Discontents*. New York: New York Ubiversity Press.

———. 1973. "The Structuralist Promise." *The British Journal of Sociology* 24(1): 67–83.

Bhabha, Homi K. 1982. "Signs Taken for Wonders: Questions of Ambivalence and Authority under a Tree outside Delhi, May 1817." *Critical Inquiry* 12(1): 144–165.

———. 1990. *Nation and Narration*. New York: Routledge.

———. 1992. "Freedom's Basis in the Indeterminate." *October* 61: 46–57.

———. 1992. "The World and the Home." *Social Text* 31/32: 141–153.

———. 1998. "'On the Irremovable Strangeness of Being Different.' From 'Four Views on Ethinicity.'" *PMLA* 113(1): 28–51.

Chatterjee, Partha. 1996. *Mapping the Nation*. Edited by G. Balakrishnan. London: Verso.

Cudd, Ann E. 2004. "The Paradox of Liberal Feminism." In *Varieties of Feminist Liberalism*, edited by A Baehr, 191–203, New York, NY: Rowman and Littlefield.

Gashé, Rodolphe. 1989. "Infrastructures and Systematicity." In *Deconstruction and Philosophy: The Texts of Jacques Derrida*. Edited by John Sallis, 3–20. Chicago: University of Chicago Press.

Hemmings, Clare. 2011. *Why Stories Matter: The Political Grammar of Feminist Theory*. Durham, NC: Duke University Press.

Hutchinson, Allan C. 1992. "Doing the Right Thing? Towards a Postmodern Politics." *Law and Society Review* 26(4): 773–788.

Marotta, Vince. 2002. "Zygmunt Bauman: Order, Strangerhood and Freedom." *Thesis Eleven* 70(1): 36–54.

Sartre, Jean-Paul. *Being and Nothingness*. Translated by Hazel E. Barnes. New York: Washington Square Press, 1966.

Smith, Anthony. 1998. *Modernism and Nationalism*. New York: Routledge

Tester, Keith. 2004. *The Sociological Thought of Zygmunt Bauman*. New York, NY: Macmillian.

Walcott, Derek. 1990. *Collected Poems 1948–1984*. New York: Noonday Press.

www.ingramcontent.com/pod-product-compliance
Lightning Source LLC
Chambersburg PA
CBHW030300130626
46549CB00002B/624